Raising Kids in Today's
Digital World

Proven Positive Parenting Tips for Raising Respectful, Successful and Confident Children

Bukky Ekine-Ogunlana

...e-Ogunlana 2021 - All rights

...ent of this book may not be reproduced, duplicated, ...ransmitted without direct written permission from the author or the publisher.

Under no circumstance will any blame or legal responsibility be held against the publisher, or author, for any damages, reparation, or monetary loss due to the information contained within this book. Either directly or indirectly. You are responsible for your own choices, actions, and results.

Legal Notice:

This book is copyright protected. This book is only for personal use. You cannot amend, distribute, sell, use, quote, or paraphrase any part, or the content within this book, without the consent of the author or publisher.

Disclaimer Notice:

Please note the information contained within this document is for educational and entertainment purposes only. All effort has been executed to present accurate, up-to-date, and reliable, complete information. No warranties of any kind are declared or implied. Readers acknowledge that the author is not engaging in the rendering of legal, financial, medical, or professional advice. The content within this book has been derived from various sources. Please consult a licensed professional before attempting any techniques outlined in this book

By reading this document, the reader agrees that under no circumstances is the author responsible for any losses, direct or indirect, which are incurred as a result of the use of the information contained within this document, including, but not limited to,—errors, omissions, or inaccuracies.

Published by
TCEC Publishing
TCEC House
14-18 Ada Street, London Fields,
E8 4QU, England, Great Britain.

Table of Contents

Raising Girls in Today's Digital World: 7

    Introduction 8

    Chapter 1: Raising Girls 11

    Chapter 2: The Early Years... 24

    Chapter 3 Developmental Milestones............................ 35

    Chapter 4: Cultivating Creativity.................................. 46

    Chapter 5: Building Strong Relationships with Your Daughter.. 63

    Chapter 6: Ambition and Education............................. 87

    Chapter 7: The Internet...90

    Chapter 8: The Joy of Raising Daughters 99

    Please leave a 1-click Review!................................... 106

    Conclusion 107

Raising Boys in Today's Digital World:................................ 110

    Introduction 111

    Chapter 1: Challenges of Raising Sons 121

    Chapter 2: Core Values...129

    Chapter 3: Raising Sons as a Single Parent.................... 147

    Chapter 4: Mentoring Boys 160

    Chapter 5: How raising boys differ from girls...............176

    Chapter 6: A Hard Hill to Climb 192

Chapter 7: The Joy of Raising Sons 203

Please Leave a 1-click Review! 211

Conclusion 212

Other Books You'll Love! 214

References 219

Dedication

This book is dedicated to our three amazing children and all the beautiful children worldwide who have passed through the T.C.E.C 6-16 years program over the years. Thank you for the opportunity to serve you and invest in your colorful and bright future.

Raising Girls in Today's Digital World:

Proven Positive Parenting Tips for Raising Respectful, Successful and Confident Girls

Introduction

Girls are often viewed as the gentle and more sensitive counterpart to boys. As a result, parents often feel pressure to raise their daughters very differently than their sons for this reason. However, while there are quite a few obvious differences between boys and girls, each gender tends to undergo its own set of challenges, which is why parents must be prepared to face these challenges. This book is accompanied by other parenting books geared explicitly for raising boys in this age group. Refer to those books for a comprehensive guide on how to raise well-rounded boys.

The first few chapters of this book will feature a list of developmental milestones that serve as a checklist for raising their daughters. These checklists can also be applied for sons as well. Many parents tend to feel pressured by such checklists, especially if their child is not hitting some of these milestones for their age group. These checklists serve as a guideline and are not necessarily the universal standard for raising your children. Every child is different and experiences different circumstances due to their upbringing and environment. If your child is not hitting these milestones at the age of four years old, for example, aim to teach them and help them develop the skills to build these skills as they age.

Rather than put pressure on parents, these checklists serve as some of the goals you might want to focus on when raising and spending time with your daughters. Teaching children about how the world works is an incredibly overwhelming feat. Many parents turn to parenting books such as this to develop a structure that works for their busy schedules and their children's increasingly busy lives to raise their kids in an organized way that is hitting all of the essential points they need to make. These checklists are an excellent way to track their child's progress and identify areas they might even struggle with for many parents. For example, many parents find that their children might be working with the social aspect of communication because they are timid and afraid of meeting new people. This can be an excellent way to figure out how to get your child to meet new people and get more comfortable making friends and socializing with their peers.

Ultimately, these books serve as a guide for parents, rather than being a means of pressuring and shaming them if they are not hitting all of the points mentioned in these books. These books guide parents down an efficient and organized path when it comes to raising their children. These books take out many of the challenges that parents face raising kids as they come to terms with teaching their children about how the world works and how we are shaped by our immediate environment and the people around us.

After reading this guide, please feel free to leave a review based on your findings and how valuable the guide was to you. I would be incredibly thankful if you could take 60 seconds to write a brief review on Amazon or the platform of purchase, even if it's just a few sentences!

Chapter 1:
Raising Girls

You may be thinking or wondering, "How can I raise my daughter to be the best version of herself?" This starts by acknowledging that there are quite a few differences between girls and boys, especially young girls and boys between the age group of three and twelve. During this time, your child will go from preschool to kindergarten and will begin elementary school. These are the years when they will experience the differences imposed on various genders due to stereotypes and stigmas associated with being male or female.

Boys will often be treated as stronger, more athletically capable, braver, and sometimes even smarter. For girls, they are often treated as sensitive, afraid, and delicate damsels in distress. Teachers and parents often encourage this perception who might feel the need to treat girls like babies continuously. When it comes to girls, parents tend to adopt a more helicopter parenting style, which isn't necessarily a good thing but can undoubtedly present its own set of cons for your daughter's development. Parents tend to fall into this mindset that their daughters are much more delicate and softer than their sons, making them worry even more for their daughters than they would for their sons. This mindset is dangerous for raising girls because it teaches them that they are not fully capable of independence and thinking for themselves. Girls are incredibly complex, and just like boys, they can be strong, courageous, and athletic as much as boys of their age are. While you might believe this and resist gender stereotypes within your household, your daughters might find that their peers or their teachers at school will not feel the same way. This is why when you are raising your daughter, you should always have the mindset of telling them that they are as capable as they want to be. Raising your children to prepare them for such challenges that society will throw at them is one of the most important lessons taken away from these books.

From birth to twelve years old, these years are often regarded as the "discovery years." These are the preliminary years where your child will explore the world around them and try to make sense of the new people and faces they are constantly seeing. They will be coming to terms with the new sensations, sights, and sounds that the world throws at them. These are the first years into your child's development as a fully-fledged functioning member of society. The ages before three are when your daughter will take her first few steps, form her first sentences, and learn the fundamental differences between "yes" or "no" or even "good" and "bad." During these years, your child is undergoing the basic levels of child development. These are the years where you want to set your child up for physical and emotional development. The years coming after these will be even more complex and intricate for your child to navigate as they have to communicate, think, and socialize more than they ever have as they leave the household sphere and explore the world that exists outside.

Many experts will say that the first five years of a child's life are crucial and critical for their success and development for the rest of their lives. This certainly rings true because these early experiences and childhood memories will carry forward for the rest of their lives, both consciously and subconsciously. In the earlier years, the primary purpose for your child is to learn and develop regularly. This is done through toys and stimulations like books and videos and the various people that come in and out of their lives. This is also the chance for parents to focus on the influences on their child's lives. During this time, physical activity, health, and community can be set up in your child's life so that they can understand that these connections are going to follow them into their future. These skills are critical because your child learns how to navigate their own emotions and preferences as you set up various experiences for your child. The preliminary stages are when they get used to the security that you have provided them. They will learn the differences between laughter and crying and understand the concept of love.

The relationships that they are surrounded by, particularly between mother and father, will help your daughters understand that connections drive human beings and bring them together. These are the foundations of human behavior and social communication that your child will need to succeed, especially when entering the school system. These are the ages where your child will begin to understand authority in their lives. They will start to see their parents, grandparents, aunts, uncles, and older siblings as role models and mentors in their lives. They will look to these more senior people to form their behavior and attitudes towards things.

Maria was a new mother who was also a stay-at-home mom to her daughter Lucy. She found herself having difficulty coming to terms with parenthood, even though Lucy was almost four years old. This manifested within their household as Maria was somewhat disorganized with her everyday tasks and raising Lucy at the same time. Her husband James worked long hours as a lawyer and did not spend as much time with Lucy.

Maria was hit to realize that she couldn't do things entirely on her own and needed support. As much as she wanted her husband to be her support system, he was not readily available as she had hoped. This resulted in her relying on the people around her to help raise Lucy, where she reached out to her sisters for help and guidance on how to raise her daughter. The important thing was that Maria sought help. Especially during the critical years of your child's life, you want to be able to rely on the resources around you so that you don't jeopardize these essential years. For Maria, she was a mentor to her child, but she also realized that she needed to take some time off for her mental health and well-being. As a result, Maria had to put her foot down and convey to her husband that he needed to step in more so that Lucy had a balance between both parents and wasn't wholly reliant on Maria herself. Having Maria's sister Anne come down often to babysit

Lucy was an excellent way for Maria to recharge and reset, giving Lucy a fair chance at having an organized and structured life.

During these critical years, your child will need a lot of stimulation from toys and their people. Most of the time, one parent cannot simply do all of it and require a break-in juggling various responsibilities. Rather than trying to take everything on at once, try working out a schedule for your child and yourself so that a parent can take some time for themselves to complete the million other things that they have to get done for the day. This was also a wake-up call for James, who realized that Lucy struggled because of the lack of balance within their household. Because he had left all the child-rearing to Maria, Lucy was falling behind on some of the developmental milestones that she should have been hitting by four years old. For example, by the age of four, your child should respond to people outside the family. However, when Lucy was taken to play dates with other cousins, she wasn't interested in responding to friends or socializing. As new parents, James and Maria sought professional advice because they were initially very concerned when they realized that Lucy was falling a little behind. Of course, falling behind on these checklists is not necessarily a bad thing. Still, for James and Maria, they realized that she did not have a reliable daily routine because of the daily chaos from Maria taking everything on at once. This also does not mean that Maria was a bad parent by any means.

On the contrary, it makes her a fantastic parent because she realized her limitations and wanted the best for her girl, so she sought out help to begin with. Many parents might feel ashamed or afraid, especially single parents, when it comes to reaching out and using the resources at their disposal because they fear that they will be seen as inferior, less efficient, and incapable. But the truth and reality are that it takes a village to raise a child, so relying on your community around you to give your child the best childhood experience possible is an effective strategy.

These are also the years you explain some of the most fundamental values, such as patience and hard work, to your daughter. Even with simple toys that toddlers are playing with, such as building blocks or dolls, these pose as fantastic opportunities for parents to not only create a bond with their child as they spend more time with them, but this is also the time to start teaching the basic mechanics of being patient when they want something—for example, teaching your daughter to wait as you are completing a task by teaching her the concept of patience. Another effective way to teach such a big concept is by allocating specific times for playtime that your child must adhere to, to understand that not everything happens simply because they want it. For example, as much as they might want to play with their toys at bedtime, they need to realize that bedtime means quiet activities like reading. These can seem like extremely complex concepts to be teaching a toddler. Still, the reality is that implementing these concepts from a young age is what gets your children to easily identify these lessons when they age so that it didn't become so much of a chore because it is simply a part of life.

When we previously discussed the story about Lucy and her parents, we touched on developmental milestones. This can be a bit controversial because certain parents might feel defensive if their child is not hitting a particular set of milestones by a certain age. The first thing that is important to know is that not every child will experience the same thing, and not every child will undergo the same rate of development. If your child is falling behind in getting such milestones, this is by no means a cause for alarm or an immediate concern that something serious is afloat. For Maria and James, who were new parents at the time, they were highly concerned with everything Lucy did because this was unfamiliar territory. But by the time the couple had their second and third child, they realized that all children learn at different rates, and it was an even worse idea to put pressure on their child to be picking up things as quickly as their sibling or their peers. Your first daughter might be quick to pick up cognitive skills that include thinking and problem-solving. For example, at the age of four years old, your daughter might be able to identify a handful of colors and be able to understand the concept of "same" and "different." But, at the same time, another child who is also four years old might be able to count to a higher number or play a more complex game of pretending. Some children might not even be as advanced when it comes to cognitive learning. Some kids might be more developed in movement and physical activity where they can hop, chase after balls, and have the better hand-eye coordination to do essential arts and crafts. These milestones are significant, of course, but it's not necessarily something to stick to a very strict timeline when it comes to raising your children. You should be able to hit a couple of these milestones around the age of four, but they also have all of the next few years to pick up these little skills, especially when they hit the school-age to focus on practicing these abilities even more.

As your child ages a little bit, you might choose to enroll them in a preschool. These classes are typically for kids aged around three years old. Some parents might think that sending their children to preschool is a way to get them trained on all of the basic skills that they will need. This, however, is a common misconception. Instead, preschool is a time for them to socialize and practice the basic skills they have developed. Your child at this age should be potty trained and should be able to separate themselves from you for a few hours at a time weekly. This preschool age is especially great for parents looking to get their daughters into socializing with other children. Interacting with other children is an excellent way for them to learn social interaction and cooperation that you might not provide in the household because you don't have many other children available to socialize with your child. Preschool is mainly focused on communication, and while you can plant the first few seeds of teaching your children how to speak and convey their feelings, communication truly blooms at preschool. Preschool is a time to interact with other kids of their age and express themselves in social settings.

Preschool is by no means a requirement, but this depends on the laws based on where you live. Some parents may believe that preschool is mandatory, while others will argue that it is not a necessity. Regardless of where you are or fall on the spectrum, preschool is a great way to drive home some of the basic skills that you have taught your children and allow them to expand on them. Because these are some incredibly critical years, you want your child to have structure and a reliable schedule that sometimes busy parents might not be able to provide. If you find that you fall under this category, consider sending your child to preschool because they will be able to interact with students and teachers while also practicing some cognitive, mental, and physical skills that will teach them logic, focus, and rational thinking. In academics, your child will be introduced to their ABCs and learn the basics of writing their name and even address. This also teaches your child independence, which is another essential factor that you want to focus on when raising a toddler that is also touched upon later in this guide.

Developmental Milestones (Age Three to Four Years Old)
Social and Emotional
They should play make-believe games to develop their scenarios and incorporate characters like mom and dad. Kids are also beginning to create social connections and would rather play with other children than by themselves. Your child is also able to

cooperate and share with their friends. When it comes to expressing themselves, your child can talk about their likes and dislikes in simple yet effective sentences. Kids are also fearless at this age and will typically enjoy exploring new things and being curious about the world around them.

Language and Communication
Your child will understand the difference between "he" and "she." They can sing simple nursery rhymes or poems such as *The Wheels on the Bus*. They will discuss their favorite things and may even carry simple conversations by continuously asking questions.

Cognitive Learning
At this age, kids can identify basic name colors and a few numbers. They are growing increasingly familiar with the concept of time and are understanding the beginnings of counting numbers. Kids should be comfortable playing games with other people, with dolls, blocks, Legos, etc. When it comes to reading comprehension, they will understand plots of age-appropriate books and might even suggest what might happen next and further on in the story.

Physical Development

Your child can hop, skip, and jump. In addition, their hand and eye coordination are improving as they can catch balls in games.

Chapter 2:
The Early Years

When you are first raising your daughter from infant to toddler, these years mainly focus on helping your child thrive and learn the essential functions of being a human. Once they hit age three, however, this is when it becomes crucial to begin shaping them into the people who will find their place in society. These early years are challenging because parents find it hard to navigate through their newfound role as a parent and how to cope with the everyday challenges of their children growing. Children during this time are growing at a rapid rate as they explore the world around them and are curious about everything. Girls don't quite have a concept of good and bad, and these are the early stages that are crucial for parents to teach their young kids.

The age of five is when your child will be experiencing some more complex social emotions as they are likely going to preschool and meeting new people. Eventually, they will be going to kindergarten, where the stakes will be even higher as they meet even more students. Your child will be exposed to different people around them, and they will see the different dynamics that make up social relations around them. Within this age group, social interaction is significant, and these are also the years that will set them up for their social and emotional range in the future.

Developmental Milestones (Age: Five Years Old)
Social and Emotional
Your child would have made some friends that they frequently see during this time. At this age, they are looking to please their friends, and sometimes, they might even want to be like their friends in terms of mannerisms and behavior. This is the time to lookout for behavior that your child may never have exhibited before. This is when peers are going to have a direct influence on your child's behaviors and attitudes.

The concept of rules is also becoming more and more common in your child's life. As a result, your child is more likely to agree with school and household rules and understand that they need to respect their elders' authority.

They should also tell the difference between real life and the fictional worlds they see on TV or in books.

This is also a time where independence is flourishing. They may feel confident enough to make new friends at school or even visit the next-door neighbor to play alone without their parents constantly being around.

This is also a phase when your child can be very demanding and might still struggle with dealing with their emotions when they're frustrated, angry, or sad.

Language
By this time, your child should be speaking quite clearly. They should be able to form a complete sentence that makes sense and follows a pattern of logic. Grammatically, your child will be able to understand future tense and will be able to make a story that has a cohesive beginning, middle, and end. This is also when your child should be able to state their full name and address. This is an important safety measure that all parents should take when it comes to raising your child.

Cognitive

Your child will be able to count to 10 and might even go beyond that. They will be able to identify a few letters and numbers but may struggle with mixing up some of the shapes of their letters. They will be able to copy basic shapes like triangles and draw them out from memory.

Physical

Your child at this time should be able to use a fork and spoon by this age with little difficulty. This is also the period when your child will be able to use the toilet independently and will not have to rely on an adult to go to the bathroom. The age of five is also usually a very active age where your child will be able to do somersaults, climb up the playground, and play for an extended period.

At the age of five, parents are also looking to break some of the habits that your child may have developed as babies. The primary practice that parents are looking to break at the age of five years old is thumb sucking or finger sucking. Finger sucking can be a tough habit for a child to break. Usually, by the age of five or six, children naturally stop sucking their fingers. But sometimes, parents might feel like they don't see the signs of them stopping. This usually isn't a significant issue unless your child's permanent teeth are starting to come in. This is when thumb sucking can seriously affect the development of their teeth and lead to the risk of having dental problems. When it comes to addressing sucking habits, some experts say that they need to be tackled at around three.

On the other hand, some parents say that the age of five is an excellent time to encourage your child to stop sucking their thumbs. This is one of the significant challenges that parents are looking to tackle yet cannot navigate. When it comes to explaining to their child that this habit needs to stop, sometimes it takes a simple explanation for a child to stop doing something they comprehend and practice. However, more likely than not, kids will have difficulty grasping why they need to stop something they find comfort in. If your child is tenacious and uncooperative, here are some strategies that you might involve when you are trying to encourage your child to stop any habit. These steps can also be applied to other habits such as wetting the bed as well.

1. Positive reinforcement: This is one of the most commonly tried and tested parenting methods and continues to be used today. It is an excellent way to encourage your child to do something without making them feel bad or ashamed of their habits. Praising them or even

rewarding them with small perks like an extra bedtime story or a treat is an excellent way to give them something to look forward to that encourages them to stop their habit. Positive reinforcement can be as simple as you would like or be taken to another level by incorporating a calendar. Some parents enjoy creating a chart or a graph for their child. These can be as easy and simple as a daily habit tracker for your kids to show them their progress. By setting goals, you can create a visual aid for your child to refer to whenever they struggle to break their habit. Stickers are a fun way to record your child's behavior and show them how well they are doing.

2. Identify triggers: Sometimes, these habits persist, especially when your child is younger, because of specific stressors or triggers. Identify why your child is still seeking comfort through sucking their fingers. Sometimes they might need extra reassurance or attention that they may not be receiving, and it may just be as straightforward as giving them few words of comfort or spending a little more time with them. You might even consider teaching your child a different way to cope with their emotions. Maybe they might feel like they want to express themselves and are unable to. They

may feel overwhelmed with emotions that their body triggers them to seek comfort from their habit, so try talking to them and talking through their feelings to try and grasp what they may be feeling to stop relying on their practice to self-soothe.

3. Offer a gentle reminder: Your child is prone to forgetting that their habit needs to be broken. If you catch them sucking their finger, instead of criticizing them, offer a gentle reminder to don't have negative feelings towards authority and be told what to do. Rather than scolding them or even blaming them, you want to be able to guide them gently so that they don't feel ashamed or afraid.

4. Don't put too much pressure: Because every child is incredibly different, some kids might easily give up finger sucking, while others might find that their child is having a challenging time breaking the habit. As much as you explain to your child the reason to stop, they may not completely understand, or they may even suck their thumb without thought. Try not to put much pressure on your child because it may cause them to feel anxious or stress them out because you are constantly looking for them to make mistakes. This can, in turn, delay the entire process of them giving up

a habit that they might give up naturally over time. Remember that hobbies like thumb sucking often stop as your child ages. Instead of being extremely militant, a good strategy is reminding them and watching their behavior for a little bit before taking a break if you feel like progress isn't being made. Constantly focusing on their need to break a habit can have the opposite effect.

5. Seek professional help: For parents who are highly concerned, you might be able to speak to your dentist about conveying to children that thumb sucking needs to stop. Sometimes talking to a doctor or dentist and having your child present for the conversation will teach them that it's not just mum or dad being annoying or overprotective.

6. Use tools: For kids who need a bit more guidance regarding thumb-sucking, consider using a finger guard. Tools like the TGuard are simple plastic guards that take out the pleasure from thumb sucking, thus leading kids to break the habit.

When it comes to wetting the bed, approximately 15% of children wet the bed at 5. As kids age, this number decreases. Boys are twice as more likely to soak the mattress compared to girls. For parents trying to tackle this problem, you might want to begin by examining *why* your children wet the bed. Some of the common reasons that children wet the bed can be attributed to:

- Sleep: Some children are extremely deep sleepers, to the point where they miss their bodily cues and might not be able to wake up in the middle of the night to go to the bathroom. Another reason relating to sleep could be that children might be having disturbed or poor sleep, which results in having a more profound sleep because they are exhausted.
- Stress: Bed wetting can result when children are going through significant life changes, stressing them out. This can be something like moving house or a new addition to the family like a sibling. These reasons can often lead to children wetting the bed due to these significant changes in their life.
- Time: Some kids need extra time to understand their bodily changes. Parents might feel like their kids should not be wetting the bed at a certain age, but ultimately every child is different and will undergo a different development course.
- Medical issues: Sometimes, the reason for bed wetting can be a little bit more serious. Some kids might have difficulty staying dry because they are experiencing the symptoms of

medical conditions such as a urinary tract infection. The best and most appropriate way to address an issue like this is by speaking to your child's doctor. This is usually a rare case, but if you find that none of your methods and interventions seem to be working, consulting your doctor might be the next step for you.

For parents who are looking to reduce bed wetting and train their children to stay dry throughout the night, here are some tips that you can try:

- Reduce drinks before bed and avoid giving your child fizzy drinks and caffeine. This can lead to increased thirst.
- Encourage your kids to use the bathroom before they go to bed to go to sleep comfortably and not have to wake up in the middle of the night to use the bathroom.
- Sometimes your child will not wake up in the middle of the night because they are simply not used to the bodily cues telling them to go to the bathroom. This can result from them not having enough sleep, so make sure to encourage your children to sleep early. Furthermore, encourage them to restful sleep by removing distractions like electronics, games, and pets from their room when it's time for bed.

- An essential thing to remember is to avoid punishing your child if they do have an accident. Remember that they cannot control this and as much as it can be frustrating, training your children is a work in progress. Punishing them or raising your voice at them only increases their stress and makes them feel ashamed of something that they may not be able to help. Instead, help your child clean up and help them reset so that they can keep trying to break their habit.
- Keep track of your children's habits by marking a calendar or creating a chart of every time they have an accident. This will show them their progress and will also be a motivating factor for them to see how well they have been doing. You might also be able to identify any patterns and notice when their bed wetting is getting worse or better.

Chapter 3
Developmental Milestones

By the age of six, your child establishes their own pace in life and should be comfortable going to school. They should have an everyday schedule where they meet their friends, teachers, peers, and family. By the age of six, kids are generally developing at a steady rate and are advancing into learning new ways to express themselves and understand the world around them.

Developmental Milestones (Age: 6 Years Old)
By this age, kids will be experiencing some new dynamics within social relationships in terms of emotional and social development. At the age of six, kids tend to want to feel "big," and they might feel the need to be more independent or appear capable by themselves. Kids are going to have typical fears, such as monsters and big animals. They might also seek

more attention and engagement from parents because they are getting more advanced in playing, speaking, and communicating with their people. Often, parents will find that their six-year-old will want to have a rambunctious and active play. Still, parents may not consistently deliver because kids around this age are very involved with unmatched energy levels. Another significant development at this age is that they start to empathize with the people around them. They grasp that the people around them have feelings, too, and they will relate to negative feelings around them. More importantly, while they are still focused on themselves, they are also beginning to learn that others can feel negative emotions like shame, embarrassment, and sadness which they can be the cause of.

Language Development

Kids should be able to explain and describe their favorite TV shows or movies. Although they previously were able to form simple sentences, they became comfortable sharing simple stories from beginning to end and may even include different aspects of the story. In terms of grammar, kids around this age speak more accurately, and they can also read essential words.

Motor Development

Kids are working on getting control over their major muscles, and they are going to be spending a lot of time running, jumping, skipping, hopping, and other forms of physical play that involve using their bodies. Their hand and eye coordination are improving, and many parents choose to enroll their children in sports around this age because they will be able to cope with the demands of various sports. They will also be able to dress. At the age of six, kids are beginning to develop some of their own strong opinions, and dressing might be one of the first few ways that you can use to instill this sense of independence.

One of the essential things that you must address as a parent from an early age is laziness. Laziness can manifest at a very early age if parents are not proactive in getting their children engaged with their environment and the people around them. Kids have a lot of energy in them, but kids may not understand the importance of using their time productively if not channeled into the proper sport or activity. Often, parents might be tempted to let the television or video games babysit their children. Busy schedules and hectic lives can take a parent away from watching their children all the time, which is how technology slowly crept into the lives of children and relied on to keep them distracted and entertained. However, this can have incredibly detrimental effects. For one, your child will not be going outside and experiencing the environment, which gives them a lot of health benefits.

This was certainly the case for Amanda, who was six years old and just beginning to enter preschool. Preschool ended up being a massive shock to her because her mother, who was extremely busy with her work, had allowed Amanda to spend hours entertaining herself by watching TV movies and playing games on her iPad. Amanda's mum found that when her daughter entered preschool, it was a tough transition because Amanda was unprepared for the different challenges that came her way. For the other students, preschool was a natural next step in their development. For someone like Amanda, she was unprepared to cooperate and communicate with other students and was unequipped with some of the basic skills that you would need for preschool and kindergarten. Even though Amanda's mother worked at home, Amanda was usually left to entertain herself as her mother was busy running her business. So, Amanda and her mother didn't have much time to focus on teaching her the essential communication skills that would be expected of a 6-year-old. For example, Amanda was not cooperative with her teachers when she went to kindergarten because she had not been taught to listen and respect authority figures. Another major challenge that Amanda had to face was the fact that she was very lazy. While all the kids loved playing games together and getting active outside on the playground, Amanda preferred to spend her time pleading with her teacher to allow her to stay indoors and avoid having to run around and be active. For Amanda's mother, this was a big wake-up call because she realized that she had not been spending enough time with her daughter and relied on kindergarten to teach her daughter the things that were her responsibility. Luckily, Amanda was still very young at this point and was still able to break her habits and replace them with better, healthier habits. Over time, as Amanda went to school more and got to know her peers, she became more enthusiastic about socializing with her friends. Amanda's mum implemented new rules into Amanda's daily life by limiting Amanda's time to spend on her electronics. Instead, they spent more time together by taking up gardening. Together, they worked on planting new flowers outside. They were able to bond, and Amanda found that she was more excited to spend time away from her iPad. Amanda's mother had quickly learned her mistakes and implemented new measures to effectively reset her daughter and teach her a different way of life. Kids can soon pick up new things at this age and are open to new ideas, which is why it's crucial always to examine your kid's habits and make sure that they are on the right path.

It can be a huge challenge to try and combat bad habits when it comes to having lazy kids because things like the TV and iPads entertain your children for hours on end. Children need the right motivation so that they are not acting lazy all the time. There are also a lot of reasons as to why your child might be acting sluggish. Sometimes, sluggish behavior can indicate more profound behavioral and mental challenges that your child cannot cope with.

1. Kids might be using being lazy as an excuse. For example, some kids might say that they are too lazy to do something when they are too scared to give something their best shot because they fear failure. They don't want to be judged for their performance, and as a way of getting out of doing something, they end up claiming that they are "too lazy."
2. Being lazy is also another excuse that kids use as an attempt for attention. This seems to be the case when kids are young particularly, and they feel neglected because they may not understand that parents have to spend time away from them to work or take care of other siblings. When kids constantly excuse feeling

lazy, their concerned parents will then be giving them attention to make them stop their habit.
3. Correlating with the second point, children sometimes want parents to wait on them hand and foot constantly. By acting lazy, parents might feel compelled to work extra hard to give the kids exactly what they want because they feel guilty over seemingly neglecting their kids. Kids might be lazy by requesting their parents to do things that they are fully capable of doing themselves.

Once you have identified why your child may be feeling lazy, here are some methods that you might want to adopt when it comes to helping them handle their laziness.

1. Teach your children the value of things. For example, if you were trying to encourage them to spend time outside, teach them that spending time outside will have many benefits. They might not see your point from the get-go, but taking the time to just explain to them why it's not beneficial to spend time indoors can show them that they may have less free time as they age, which is why they need to take advantage of the free time they have now.

2. Teach them about privilege. Things like watching TV and spending time on the iPad are privileges that many children do not have access to. Instill within your children that privileges are earned. For example, if you find out that your child is spending way too much time being lazy, taking advantage of their screen time, and not being productive, giving your kids chores and other responsibilities for them to complete to earn privileges is a good lesson to instill in them from a young age.

3. Be an example to your children. This is one of the biggest takeaways from these guidebooks. As a parent, your child is always looking towards you for guidance on behaving and acting. Before you look to them to figure out why they might be exhibiting lazy behavior, always look at your habits first. Their habits might have been something that they have picked up from you. It's always important to look at yourself before you look at your child and try to correct him on their behavior. The last thing you will want to do is be a hypocrite. Instead, examine your behavior and see if you are constantly lazy. If you are trying to change those habits, involve your child in your efforts so that they can see that change is possible. They will also learn that both adults and

children can continuously evolve and become a better version of themselves.

4. Make a habit of being proactive. Volunteering and sharing in your community is an excellent way to get your child involved outside. From as young as five years old, teaching your children to be productive within their community sets them up to be active citizens. Encouraging your child to think beyond themselves is an excellent way to prevent laziness overall. Allowing your child to volunteer at events in your community or attending group play dates with their peers is a perfect way to motivate them to think about other people and making a positive impact on their lives. As they age, consider sending them to volunteer in the community by planting trees, helping out at a local food bank, or cleaning up beaches. By making this, a habit will encourage your child to look forward to these events and help them feel more like they are a part of something bigger than themselves.

5. At this young age, teach your children essential responsibilities by getting them involved in household management. Whether it's in the kitchen by asking them to help make dinner or with daily chores by giving them primary responsibilities. These little habits will motivate

them to get things done. For example, children who are six years old and are still very young, teach to clean up after themselves or help set the table at dinner time. These are minimal tasks that are simple for them to do but will show them that they also play a major significant role in the household, which motivates them to be less lazy and perform their duties as part of the family.

6. The most effective way to prevent laziness is by helping your kids learn the value of life. Encourage their curiosity about the outdoors by planning activities outside with the family to lighten their mood and encourage them to spend time in Mother Nature. Gardening is a simple activity that you can do with your child to teach them basic biology and get them to engage with their environment.

Everyone has lazy days, and there is nothing wrong with that. Convey to your child that it is normal to have rest days because sometimes life can get extremely hectic and stressful, even at their young age, as they balance the different activities you have planned for them. Avoid judging and criticizing them for their behavior. Instead, choose to examine why they feel lazy. Perhaps they feel like they don't have any friends, and no one wants to play with them. By figuring out why your child may be overly lazy and highly dependent on screen time are good ways to start tackling this behavior so that you can guide them to live a more proactive and curious life. Figure out activities that capture their interest. For example, if your child once enjoyed drawing, perhaps they need something a little bit different to pique their interest, such as painting. Maybe they have lost interest in that hobby and require something entirely different, like dance or picking up an instrument. Children are like sponges. This is because they soak up everything around them, so they should constantly be stimulated by various activities. This serves to challenge their mental capabilities and give them a new skill set from which they will learn new lessons that they can take with them for the rest of their lives. When it comes to laziness, it takes a lot of action to combat this habit. Parents need to be at the forefront of this action so that their young children can realize that this behavior is bad for their mental health and stability also stunts their developmental growth.

Chapter 4:
Cultivating Creativity

You might feel tempted to limit your daughters to a specific set of hobbies or sports because society says so. For example, extracurriculars like dance and art tend to be catered towards girls because they are seen as more feminine than sports like soccer or football, which are typically regarded as "masculine hobbies." This severely limits your child's capabilities because it forces them to conform within a particular box that is their gender. Rather than adhering to this way of thinking, you want to be able to give your child all the possible means to cultivate their creativity so that they can reach their fullest potential.

Allow your daughter to explore whatever sparks her interests. Encouraging her to be curious about the things around her and to ask questions is an excellent way to encourage her to cultivate her creativity. Sometimes you might find that your kids are asking so many questions that you don't know the answers to; this is a good way for you and your child to learn together to figure out the correct answers to their questions.

Provide them with the resources that they need for creative expressions. This can be as easy and simple as a blank piece of paper with a handful of crayons or something more elaborate like sending them to professional dance classes. In addition, buying books with different subject matters from dinosaurs to space to under the sea can broaden their horizons much more and teach them about exploring the world. Another good way to do this is when family and friends ask you what they should purchase for your child's birthday, encourage them to buy various things that are not necessarily marketed towards their gender and age, such as art supplies or building materials.

Foster a creative atmosphere by allowing your kids to brainstorm ideas and activities in the household. Allow them to make mistakes and fail at home as parents want to protect their children from making the wrong move, allowing them to experience failure for themselves, which teaches them that most things in life tend to come with consequences. Learning this on their own will instill a sense of independence and self-assurance within their choices and teach them to anticipate failure. Failure at a young age also teaches them to develop healthy coping mechanisms. Figuring these out at a young age can set the foundation for them later on in life when the stakes are higher and the consequences are harsher.

Share your own mistakes with your kids. It's no secret that kids these days learn best from example, and seeing their parents laugh at their own mistakes or errors teaches them that it's normal to make mistakes here and there. It also shows them that a failure is an option. Model healthy reactions to failure by picking yourself up and trying again. It can create a lot of pressure when you are constantly succeeding in life, so making mistakes and experiencing criticism or judgment is an excellent way to grow and learn from yourself. The only authentic way to understand this is by experiencing it yourself, but when children see their parents making mistakes, it helps humanize parents who are often seen as all-knowing and perfect. It also sets children up to think that adulthood is smooth-sailing when in reality, it is not.

Celebrate your child's creativity. Your kids will find different ways to express themselves. Their creative expression is unique to their identity, whether through art, music, writing, dance, science, or many other hobbies. Celebrate their work by proudly displaying it around the house. Not only is this good use of their projects, but it is also a good way for them to feel appreciated and valued.

Allow them the autonomy to explore whatever they want. Parents tend to feel like they need to be bossy or direct their children down a specific path, but this can only hinder their creativity because it can make them feel stifled and controlled. Not only are you creating constraints for your child, but you are also telling them to confine themselves within a particular box, which can block their accomplishments. Furthermore, this can set you up for failure because you are fostering resentment within your child as you constantly tell them they are not allowed to pursue what sparks their interests.

Raising a well-rounded child is often the primary goal that most parents have. Encourage your children to take part in active sports, as well as the arts, because both are equally as valuable. There are various debates over which is more important for a child's brain, but ultimately, having a balance is an excellent way to help your child grow mentally and physically. Encourage them to read for pleasure and not just for academics. This is a perfect time to go to the bookstore or library with your child and pick out new books. You might even want to read with your child because reading with kids is a great way to bond with them.

When it comes to problem-solving, this is another area where parents might feel like they must intervene. It can be tough to stop yourself from giving your children the solution to their problem but holding yourself back is more beneficial. Children must learn their way and figure out a solution for their situation. Parents aren't always going to be present to fix their issues for them, so take a step back and allow your kids to find their route to a viable solution. Allow them to stimulate their brain by coming up with possible solutions that they can use. Your child will undergo so many challenges in life, and these are the first steps to teaching them how to deal with the hurdles that life will throw at them.

The emphasis here is on the journey that your child takes towards cultivating a skill set. Many parents think that their child's achievements are the most important thing, and while those do hold merit, mainly when it comes to college applications, these early years are more focused on giving your child the chance to find their passions and hobbies they will enjoy. Focus more on the process of your child taking part in these activities rather than the end product. Instead of fixating on competition and being the best, consider their opinions about how much fun they had or what aspects of the activity they enjoyed. These are the years where you would start enrolling them in extracurricular activities that they will enjoy. Many children pursue the hobbies they start at a young age, well into their teen, young adult, and even adult years. For some, certain activities might not capture their interest, and you might have to continue trying out new things to find something that sticks. Rather than putting pressure on them to win trophies and medals, focus on making sure that they enjoy themselves and truly express themselves in creative and divergent ways.

You want your kids to feel free when they are creating, instead of being constricted by rules or feeling distressed because they have to come in the first place or do better than their peers. Unfortunately, parents tend to lose sight of this and choose to live vicariously through their children by pushing them into competitions. These pressures naturally come up later in their life, so when they are between the ages of three and ten years old, you want to allow them to be children.

Parents tend to forget that their children are achievements in themselves and feel like they have to compensate their parenting with their child achieving big awards and metals. Remember that these awards and medals don't define your child's worth, and you should not instill this concept of tying validation into your child's self-worth. Instead, the qualities and values that they bring with them throughout their lives are more important. The competitive nature of the adult world should not be brought into a child's life. They should be allowed to live their lives freely and innocently without fear of needing to compete with their peers. Adults fear failure, and as a result, many adults instill the same fear into their children at a young age, which severely stunts their development because they are afraid of judgment and criticism. Letting your kids fail gives them the self-confidence and experience that they need to handle more significant failures as they age. When they are at this young age, their losses will be insignificant compared to the ones that they might experience later in their teenage or adult life, which is why you should take advantage of their young age to instill some long-lasting lessons.

Focus on the process, not the result.

Parents who have a habit of overemphasizing achievements are likely to raise girls with psychological problems. Instead of focusing on achievements, consider focusing on the process. Girls who focus on constantly improving their attitude and efforts, rather than the result, end up achieving success that will last longer because they will learn the virtues of hard work and patience. So, be on the watch for opportunities to acknowledge your children's effort, attitude, and good behavior; you'll see that they will achieve great success naturally.

Many people think they'll instinctively pick up skills as they grow up. However, talent doesn't just sprout, and it involves a process. This process usually needs to be facilitated by parents. Getting things done is much more important than the result, and the process itself is what gives a good product. The process leads to the discovery of new ideas, and this is also a time when you will gather experience. Things change during the process, but the process also changes the child by allowing her to grow. The fundamental changes girls experience in terms of development make them the persons they are, so it's much more beneficial that girls' skills don't just sprout from nowhere.

Joanne's aunt Allison enrolled her in piano classes at a young age. Many parents struggle with this particular challenge in parenting because kids can grow tired of certain hobbies. Some parents arrive at a crossroads where they have to decide if they should force their kids to continue a pursuit or allow them to pursue something else. For some parents, moving them to be consistent might give them a chance at becoming great at their hobby. In Joanne's case, her aunt wanted her to be a concert pianist. Yet Joanne insisted that she wanted to quit playing the piano. For Allison, after having a long talk with her aunt, she realized that she was feeling frustrated at the moment and did not honestly want to quit piano after many years of practice. Children can sometimes be inconsistent, and for Allison, who insisted on perfection, the pressure became too overwhelming. This prompted Allison to relax and allow Joanne to pursue piano at her own will. Joanne grew to appreciate her aunt's perfectionism and understood why it was essential to excel with her motivations rather than allow her aunt to live through her vicariously. Joanne also understood the process of change itself. She saw how the love for her hobby would come and go, which was a regular part of gaining a skill. This was a crucial lesson because later in her life, she would take the same lessons with her and apply them to various situations in life.

Joanne later had a class teacher in her life who insisted on perfection, who valued the process of getting things done. She remembered her aunt and began to appreciate her insistence on the process. It had inadvertently instilled in her a sense of quality and excellence, which determined the high value of her excellent classwork and services at play times.

The process is essential, and it makes things work and teaches how to make things. Without a strategy, end products lose their value, and they become cheap. People with lousy quality don't have class. By focusing on just results, you may be grooming the terrible attitude of not valuing and respecting the process in what girls do. They could be helpful too, but ignore details. The detail is essential. Whatever you make your girl do, please pay attention to the process for your daughter because it determines the value, cost, and price your result will attract.

Charity's mum would not just provide her with a clean room. Instead, she made her go through the process. Providing a clean room gives the result, and she always made her daughter go through the process of getting the cleaning skill so that she would have the skills, but not without the process. So by process, Charity comes to acquire the needed skills.

Charity is a 10-year-old who can write, so her dad asked her to help edit his book to earn pocket money. That skill was a result of the process. It always pays. You go through a process of four years to acquire B.Sc., and the degree is yours. But if someone gives you the certificate, they have not helped you. You have the license, but without process, you have not acquired the skill the document represents. It is the process that makes the child skillful. The learning method is what will change your daughter's value and character, and that is what is needed and got.

Encouraging kids to work with their parents also gives them a chance to see why their parents always try to get them to branch out or try new things. Kids see that their parents are enthusiastic about learning a skill, and therefore can grasp the value of improving themselves and evolving as human beings.

When parents give money to kids for doing nothing, they are not helping them. They will accuse and blame you in the future when they lack needed skills. They will accuse you because you did not allow them to go through the process. You pay the price for them and shield them from the process and change that should happen to them, and they remain who they are and come back and stab you. The process will change their mindset and make children grow. During the procedure, they learn endurance, and endurance gives them stamina. The method also gives them inner content and forms children into a person of value. The technique of failing and getting up changes and makes kids a better person.

Process changes children and brings the best out of them. The process will discover their weakness and make your girl be a better person. If you give your daughter things without teaching her how to acquire them herself, she will most likely abuse them. The method teaches children self-control and makes them value even little things. The process develops prudence and frugality. It does not focus on the result. Even in working free, kids gain more in the process. We must not cut corners with children; they should be allowed to follow due process.

Physical things are liable to change; it is the invisible things that are not liable to change because they are more stable and predictable. The process goes with values, diligence, responsibility, truth, sincerity, faithfulness, and honesty; all great benefits to be taught. They are invisible but sustainable for the future. Your children may fail or make mistakes, but they will begin to do well in the process. Without process, values are lost, and everything collapses in time. Of course, things collapse when they lack a skeleton, an anchor, or structure that will hold them together. If children don't have these values, they will behave according to whatever situations dictates around them, and that's like leaving things to chance. That's not the right way to live.

Developmental Milestones (Age: 7-10 Years Old)
These years are often associated with rapid progress and development in all aspects. During this time, your kids acquire the social and physical skills that will equip

them with the ability to play and interact with other people. This is also a time where your kids are learning to get along with their peers. They may also be having disagreements with them as they have varying points of view. This is the time to teach your children how different the world is and that everyone has a different perspective. This age group is also when kids are generally developing the skills needed for more advanced reading, writing, and arithmetic. Kids tend to undergo some trouble during these aspects because their schoolwork is becoming increasingly challenging, and some kids might be prone to falling behind. At the same time, kids are also developing a sense of feeling self-conscious, which makes them ashamed and sad for falling behind, which is something to look out for with your kids.

These years are also significant for your children in terms of developing a moral conscience. This is when they develop a moral compass and apply their values and beliefs to various social situations. Your child uses the skills you initially installed, such as patience, respect, and honesty. However, these values will be tested because they will be placed in more challenging social situations. They spend increasing amounts of time at school and extracurriculars where they interact with several different adults and peers with different and sometimes conflicting points of view.

Also, this age group is at a time when independence is truly blossoming. Between the ages gap of seven to ten years old, your child may feel the need to be extra independent, exacerbated by the increased time they spend outside of the household and therefore rely less on you for guidance. This means that they become more self-reliant as they develop and maintain their friendships separate from the family. In addition, the ages between seven and ten years old are the years where they are developing an understanding of the rest of the world to grasp how big the world is. This is when they need structure and balance, which comes from parenting your child with care and gentleness while also being firm and disciplined.

Stress and worry can genuinely blossom as your child ages. They are experiencing new social interactions that can cause anxiety and mental health problems. Or, in many other cases, these interactions are planting the seeds of trauma that might reappear in their teenage and adult years. For example, by the age of ten years old, cliques are beginning to form in school. Cliques are extremely common for young girls. This age group is notorious for being the beginnings of cattiness and drama, and this is usually when young girls are beginning to understand the dynamics of their friendship. As they gain a perspective within their peer group, your child may experience gossiping and bullying, which is more common for girls. For parents, it is crucial to talk to your kids about the importance of respect. Your daughter may feel tempted to fall into peer pressure and what their other friends are doing, but taking the time to explain that bullying is unacceptable should be mandatory. These various dynamics will affect your child both socially and mentally, which is why it is so important to speak to her gently and calmly while also stressing the importance of treating others with the kindness and respect they would expect for themselves. Remember to remind your daughter that people are bound to make mistakes, and it is essential to grow from your inappropriate errors and learn to do better.

This was certainly the case with Mia, who was ten years old when she got into serious trouble at school for bullying another girl. Mia was part of a clique of close friends who had gone to kindergarten together. All the girls began taunting a new student named Diana. Diana was from a more impoverished family, and Mia and her group of friends found it funny to bully her for her cheap clothes and how she styles her hair. One of their teachers was caught, which led to them being sent to the headteacher's office for punishment. Their headteacher called all of their parents, which was a shock for Mia's mother, Joanne, who never expected her daughter to partake in such bad behavior. This is usually the case for most parents, who never want to think of their child as a bully. One of the other parents chose to deny the allegations and was incredibly defensive over her daughter. But for Joanne, after seeing the evidence from the teacher, she knew that she had failed her daughter at some point by allowing this behavior. Joanne knew that she would be a lousy parent if she did not teach Mia a lesson and choose to stay ignorant like the other parent. Joanne punished Mia by taking away her privileges. Mia was also told to apologize to Diana and write a formal apology to her family. It was humiliating for Mia, but more importantly, it stuck with her because her mother had told her off in front of the whole school. While you don't have to go to such lengths when disciplining your child, remember that you want your child to remember the conveyed lesson. For Joanne, it was a slap in the face when she learned that her daughter was partaking in bullying. It was incredibly saddening, and she was angered that her daughter chose to do such a thing. She was also disappointed in herself and questioned where she went wrong as a parent that led her daughter to act in such a way. But rather than spiraling out of control in guilt and shame, Joanne chose to work on the mistakes that had been made to fix the situation with Mia.

Children learn by example, and when they see that their parents are extremely unhappy with them, they will wonder why and want to figure out how to make them happy again. However, an important thing to remember is that this would not have worked if Joanne and Mia had a strong relationship. Their mother-daughter relationship was built on a solid foundation of trust and respect. Mia felt that she did not want to jeopardize her relationship with her mother, so she chose to accept her punishment and learn from her mistakes.

Chapter 5:
Building Strong Relationships with Your Daughter

Father-Daughter Relationships

As discussed in previous chapters, the relationships around your daughter will shape how she views the people that she will meet in her lifetime. Thus, the father-daughter dynamic and the mother-daughter dynamic are incredibly crucial to the success of a child's development. Unfortunately, this relationship often faces difficulty in the father-daughter relationship because men find it difficult to relate to their daughters as they age because they are more focused on interests that simply do not overlap with theirs. This, however, tends to be a poor excuse because it has been increasingly proven that even though you may not have similar interests, you can indeed find common ground if you put effort into finding it.

A poor father-daughter relationship results in daughters not having a trustworthy male figure that can lead to even more significant problems later on in their adult life, especially in future relationships. Father figures teach girls trust and respect from a young age, leaving a lasting impact on them for the more significant part of their lives. Fathers leave a mark on daughters by shaping how they view the opposite gender. A father figure is a good way for young girls to learn strength and protection for themselves. Fathers play a critical role in the psychological development of their daughters from the minute they are born. They contribute to a daughter's sense of self, and they end up becoming more confident and self-assured of their capabilities as they grow up. A father's influence can shape how the child interacts with other students when entering kindergarten and primary school. Having a solid relationship with their father will show them to be more assertive without necessarily being aggressive. As they meet new people, they feel better about themselves and have confidence in the new people that they let into their lives. While your daughter may not understand all these concepts at the age of 10 years old, she will inherently feel more secure in not only herself but the relationships she makes with her school friends.

So, how might a father cultivate a strong relationship with his daughter?

The important thing is to start the day she is born. Developing a relationship with your child begins the minute they enter the world. To be a constant positive force in their life, you need to be consistent. Be involved and hands-on with raising your child, rather than leaving your wife to have an active role in caring for her. Then, as she ages, she will not only view you as a significant figure in her life, but the relationship will not be forced in any way because she is used to your companionship, your presence, and your insight into life.

For fathers, treating your wife with respect and dignity is incredibly important because it reflects your behavior and shows your daughter proper conduct. Showing your daughter that you care for their mother teaches them that this is how they should expect to be treated by others when they are at that stage of their life. Children never want to see their parents fighting, especially young children, who tend to be less in control of their emotions and find it difficult to cope with problematic situations within the household.

When it comes to the relationships you cultivate within the family, be sure to embody respect and show your daughter the appropriate behavior.

While you do get involved with your child from an early age, you also want to teach her new things. Share your interests with your daughter, even if they may seem "too manly" for her. If your hobby is woodworking, be open to sharing this with your child and showing her your passion and love for your hobby. If you love a particular sport that other people might say is too violent or too physical for a young girl, let her make that choice by safely exposing her to it and sharing why you love that sport. The main thing here is to share your interests with your daughter, not to feel limited by societal pressure to conform to her gender. She also gets a chance to learn more about you and understand you as a person. Learning new skills with her father will teach your daughter confidence in the new things that she is trying out in life. She will know that facing the unknown is not something to be afraid of and is something to be celebrated. Overall, this can make a huge difference in her self-esteem as she grows older and faces different challenges that entering primary school and high school will bring.

Often, fathers and daughters don't take the time to talk to each other. Girls tend to seek out their mothers when talking about personal issues or challenges that they might be facing. During the ages between three and twelve years old, your child will not be experiencing too much emotional turmoil because they are still young and experiencing life with a very innocent and positive outlook. During this time, fathers should take the time to understand how their daughters think. Figure out their likes and dislikes. Take the time to let them speak so that they grow increasingly comfortable with sharing their point of view with you. An essential thing to remember is that when your daughter shares something private with you, it is crucial to keep that to yourself and avoid violating her privacy and trust. At the age of twelve, children are just beginning to develop their secrets, and some choose to share this with their parents. You should never break their trust unless necessary, and even then, this should be done by consulting them and discussing why you need to tell someone their secret.

Being involved with your daughter's life is more than just asking her how her day has been and how she's doing in school. For Peter, who is the father to Emma, he learned that his daughter was increasingly interested in astronomy, stars, and all things space at the age of nine. While Peter had never been interested in astronomy previously, he decided to take the time to research stars and planets to be able to talk to his daughter about them. He also wanted to be able to teach her about the things that he was learning. So, Peter took the time to take her to a planetarium, where they explored the stars and researched planets together. As a result, they could share a passion and develop their love for what they were learning. Learning a skill with someone else is always going to be an enjoyable experience. They both learned new skills by purchasing a telescope at home and shared their knowledge over the subject with each other. Peter and Emma also shared their progress, and in the process, they got to know each other even better. For Peter, he understood that the key to being an important figure in his daughter's life was taking the time to get to know her and her passions. He showed that he invested in her life and interests, which provided Emma with the support needed to navigate to changes that she was experiencing as she moved to a different school. Like moving to a new school or even going to a different grade, significant life changes can be a stressful factor in a child's life. This was an extremely anxiety-ridden time for Emma, and she turned to astronomy for stability and relaxation. With her father involved, she was able to take her mind off of things and share her fears with her father as they spent more quality time together.

A common misconception among new fathers is that their role is not as important as mothers when relating to their daughters, which is entirely false. On the contrary, both parents are essential to daughters' development because they provide them with the security they need. Furthermore, when a child can rely on both parents, they have access to a constant and trustworthy support system and are therefore less fearful of entering new stages of their lives.

Avoid treating your daughter like she is a damsel in distress. Fathers may feel tempted to treat their daughters as fragile and delicate beings, but the reality is that they are just as tough as boys. This also teaches girls that men will not come into their lives and save them when they are in trouble or crisis. Instead, girls have to be taught to fend for themselves, especially when they are young. This is an excellent way to teach them that they simply must pick themselves up and keep going when they fall, rather than waiting for someone to swoop in and save them.

One of the tasks that fathers must undergo when raising daughters is to teach them how to protect themselves. From a young age, fathers need to instill a sense of self-confidence by teaching them about the risks in the outside world and preparing them to have safety measures wherever they go. Kids around the ages of three and twelve years of age will have a bit of a difficult time understanding the dangers of the world around them because they are younger and, therefore, less experienced. Parents also don't want to risk scaring their young children about the world, but the reality is that they need to be equipped to know that not everyone will have their best interests at heart. When your daughters are at this stage in life where there are still young but experiencing new social situations beyond the household, both fathers and mothers have to work hard and be proactive about instilling a sense of "stranger danger" into their children. More importantly, parents have to teach their children to develop their gut feeling so that they know to trust their instincts whenever they are in potentially dangerous situations. Teach them about basic skills like never speaking to strangers or following them no matter what they say. These are survival skills that your children need to be equipped with to know what to do in dangerous or scary situations.

Here are some helpful tips on how to teach your children to be smart about strangers:

1. If they are ever approached by a stranger when they are alone for any reason, and they are offered a ride or treat, teach your children that it is okay to refuse by saying "no." Especially if the stranger persists, teach your

children that it is okay to scream and call for help. Never let your child feel ashamed for being scared or cautious.

2. Teach your child how to recognize trustworthy help from police officers or security guards if they are ever separated from you in public places. Ensure that they memorize your phone number and house address to seek help in emergencies.

3. It can be tough to explain the concept of danger to a child, so you want to be gentle and patient when explaining what to do in such situations. The best way to do so is by going over specific scenarios. Pose hypotheticals by asking them what they would do in certain conditions. For example, "What would you do if a grownup asked you to follow them to find their lost puppy?" These are simple scenarios that are realistic and will help teach your child how to act accordingly.

4. The best way for a parent to navigate this challenge is by planning and teaching their children how to anticipate certain situations. For example, if you are in a shopping mall and separated from your daughter, encourage her to ask for help from an employee. Not only does this teach her to be safe, but it also

teaches her never to be afraid to ask for help when she is in a scary situation.

5. Install a sense instinct by teaching your kids to trust their instincts. For example, if they feel like they feel where they don't trust a stranger who has approached them, they should have the confidence to follow their gut feeling and feel unashamed to go away from the person that is making them feel unsafe.

6. Educate your children on secrets. If anyone tells them to keep a secret, especially if an adult is telling them to keep something from their parents, this is usually a bad sign. Instead, encourage your children to speak up. More importantly, listen to your children when they speak, especially when discussing their discomfort from certain situations. As a parent, you want to decipher your child's language and understand that they are trying to convey a problem they might not fully understand. You never want to ignore the signs of abuse or harassment.

7. Teach them to consent from a young age. You kids should never be in a position to feel fear over voicing their opinions, especially when it is about their discomfort. The simplest way to explain consent to younger children is by putting it into relevant contexts for them. For

example, sometimes, people might want to hug your child. However, your child may not like to be hugged at all. Parents might frame this in the context of respect and force their children to hug someone. Instead, explain to your child that they are allowed to tell someone they don't want to be hugged and respect their wishes, rather than forcing them to do something they do not want to do.

Mother-Daughter Relationships

As previously mentioned, the mother-daughter relationship is just as crucial as the father-daughter dynamic in a child's life. A common misconception is that mothers have a better understanding of their daughters, and while this is somewhat true, this isn't necessarily as effortless as some people may think. Mothers tend to have an easier time relating to their daughters because they have undergone similar experiences in terms of gender. However, mothers need to put in just as much work into developing their relationship with their daughters. Developing a solid foundation and trust between a parent and a child can be a difficult task. Still, the responsibility primarily lies within parents to build a strong bond with their children to relate to them and understand the challenges they are facing as they experience life.

For mothers who are raising daughters, they have the responsibility of raising the next generation of girls. Mothers will better understand what daughters are going through in terms of self-esteem and building confidence. For girls between the ages of nine and twelve, children are just beginning to understand the meaning of beauty and beauty standards they are subjected to because of societal standards. This is especially when unhealthy body image ideas can cultivate, mainly because your daughter is going to school, making friends with other girls, and interacting with the various cliques and social dynamics in their environment. During this time, girls tend to enjoy gossiping, which is a slippery slope that can quickly enter into the realm of bullying. For a mother, the challenge lies in encouraging her daughter to build her confidence and develop her character to feel strongly about herself and self-worth. This begins with the mother believing in her daughter's capabilities that are beyond her beauty. One of the biggest mistakes often made from a young age is that girls are valued for their beauty only. Young boys are complimented for their strength and bravery, whereas girls are told that they look stunning or are dressed nicely. The focus is always on aesthetics rather than the qualities or values of the child. For a mother, raising her daughter by praising her beyond aesthetics is an easy fix. Talk about the qualities that your child is exhibiting that you are proud of. Focus on the fact that they are kind and honest individuals rather than beautiful or thin. It can be tempting to want to compliment a girl simply for her beauty and appearance, but instead of entirely focusing on that, you want to encourage her individuality.

The ages between nine and eleven are also when most girls begin their menstrual cycle. This is a meaningful conversation a parent must have with their daughters because they might not fully understand their bodies' changes. This can be an extremely stressful and scary time for young girls because their bodies undergo immense changes at such a rapid rate. Hormonal changes might also be contributing to their extreme emotions. For kids at this age, it can be a very sudden experience to begin their period at school and suddenly have to deal with the concept of womanhood. Unfortunately, some parents tend to forget this critical conversation they need to have with their daughters until it is too late. Luckily, teachers are usually equipped with the correct information, whether through pamphlets or health classes, to teach your daughters about periods if they haven't already been taught.

The language surrounding periods tends to be quite negative because many women tend to see periods as a "curse" or a negative part of being a female. However, when you are educating your child on their menstrual cycle, be sure to avoid such language because it creates a negative connotation when accepting that their bodies are changing and undergoing significant developmental transformations. Instead, communicate a more positive story about growing up and express how the female body can so much more.

Help your daughter feel in control of her period by educating her. An excellent way to do this is by shopping for period supplies together. From pads to tampons, some products out there to choose from might help ease the difficulty of having a period. Be hands-on when you show her how to use these products correctly. Their first instincts might tell them to be disgusted, but persist and teach your daughter basic hygiene skills like when to use a pad, how to use it, and the best hygienic practices.

Getting dads involved in the conversation is also essential. Many families tend to have closed doors or secrets, especially when it comes to different genders, but being open and talking about periods reduces girls' stigma and menstruating. Boys go through their form of puberty so that dads will relate to their daughter's changes to some degree. Involving dads into the conversation also shows them the specific period products that your child may be using, which can be helpful when moms are not always available to purchase from the store. Rather than treating periods as a shameful secret, treat them as a natural part of growing up to reduce its stigma.

You might even be met with resistance when you try to talk about menstruating with your daughter but try to encourage her to be open. Develop a connection with her because, as a mother, you have undergone the same process and can empathize with how she might be feeling at this moment. Rather than allow her to feel humiliated, bring it out in the open to show her that this simply is a natural process of life.

Francesca was nine years old when she first started her menstrual cycle. She was initially incredibly fearful of what was happening to her body. Despite having a solid relationship with her mother, she chose not to tell her mum about her period until much later. She ended up struggling by herself as she dealt with her period on her own the first few times it happened. One day, her mother discovered that she had begun her menstrual cycle after finding some dirty clothes that she had hidden. This was when she decided to sit down and have a challenging conversation about monthly periods. Francesca was initially terrified of what was happening to her body. Still, when she finally had the conversation with her mother, she was put at ease because she learned that this was completely normal, and all girls went through this experience. When she chose not to tell her mother about her period, she felt dirty and was incredibly self-conscious about the fact that she was menstruating. However, Francesca's mother was quick to reassure her that this was a natural bodily function that women experience and nothing to fear. Francesca's mother was also able to show her how to cope with her cramps. Honesty is fundamental in a relationship, and even if you think you have a strong foundation with your child, honesty might not be their first course of action. In the case of Francesca, there was a voice inside her head telling her to be ashamed and afraid to tell her mother. Francesca's mum was also honest about the biological changes that happen within the body. She chose to illustrate how the uterus shed its lining every month to show Francesca precisely what was happening within her body so that she understood that it was a process that was simply part of life. The emphasis was that this was a biological process, which helped Francesca feel much more empowered. Her mother had a very practical conversation with her by showing her the proper ways to use a pad and track her cycles, which would be helpful in the long run for her health.

Girls are beginning to develop into their bodies around this age, which means that this is the time to start wearing bras if they haven't already started. Mothers are generally tasked with teaching their daughters about these things. Relaying their personal experiences with their daughters is extremely helpful so that their daughters don't feel isolated when they are experiencing puberty. For single parents who are fathers raising daughters, this can be a difficult conversation to have. Still, there are so many experts and resources that can be referred to when helping your daughter understand the changes in her body. Puberty is never something to be ashamed of, despite kids feeling embarrassed or ashamed. For parents, this is the time to show them your support and care by providing them the guidance they need to know what to anticipate. Having a trustworthy guide in their lives helps them feel like they have control over their circumstances, even when they don't.

Body image is also another important topic for mothers who are raising their daughters. Issues relating to body dysmorphic disorder, eating disorders, and obsessive-compulsive disorders centered around body image can manifest at this age without the proper guidance through puberty and beyond. Here are some tips to encourage your daughter to be more positive and have confidence in her own body:

As previously mentioned, direct your praise away from just her appearance. You want to make a very conscious effort to do so because it can be straightforward to praise a girl for the way she looks. Instead, focus on her academic success or a recent hobby that she's taken up and the progress that she might be making in that aspect. Your daughter is a multifaceted individual, and you want to celebrate this rather than simply focusing on a very shallow aspect of her, which is the way she looks. Rather than focusing on looking good or finding happiness through her appearance, which are common stereotypes associated with girls, you want her to find confidence in her sense of self. In addition, you want her to invest in her mental health by helping her channel her skills through various hobbies, which can help her broaden her horizon and shape her individuality.

Kids will always turn to their parents for guidance and mentorship. It is still crucial for mothers to model body acceptance themselves. Rather than obsessing over the food you eat or continuously putting your appearance down, be kind to yourself and your own body because your daughter will immediately pick up on your behavior and model it herself. An essential thing for mothers to remember is that they would never want their child to be critical over her own body and continuously put herself down, so it is crucial to avoid doing so yourself. This is also where unhealthy relationships with food can begin because a mother might feel the pressure to be thin and have a damaged relationship with food herself. It is crucial for parents to constantly be self-aware and self-evaluative by examining their mental health and behaviors. For example, one of the prevalent ways for negative body image to manifest is through the way we look at food. It is prevalent for people to view certain foods as "good" or "bad." This way of thinking can be very unhealthy because it limits certain food groups and indoctrinates children into diet culture from a very young age. One example of this would be if you had pizza for dinner today, you might say that you ate "badly," which is why you don't deserve to have dessert or eat anything else for the rest of the day. These little connections can lead to more extreme thinking that can negatively affect the way food is perceived. This relationship is hazardous for children because they value food based on its calories, reflect on their weight rather than its nutrition, and treat food as fuel for their bodies. As a mother to young girls, you must be very careful with how you regard food yourself.

When raising a young daughter, you want to make sure that you are not growing a people pleaser. Your child will experience lots of peer pressure situations, and they might feel the need to forgo their values and discomfort to make other people feel happy. But you want to avoid this by encouraging your child to stand up for what they believe in and using the voice that they have. These are the beginnings of raising a daughter who is confident in herself. You want to raise your daughter so that she dreams big and is ambitious about her future. Giving your child opportunities to use her voice and make her own choices is planting the seeds of her confidence and self-assuredness.

Above all, for fathers and mothers alike, you want to make sure that your daughter knows that she is loved and much appreciated for who she is. Her appearance may change, her interests may fizzle out, and she may do poorly in certain areas of academics but knowing that her parents will always be there as a source of strength and comfort will lead her down a positive path of self-improvement and happiness. Teach them that love is not conditional by loving your children freely without holding back, regardless of their achievements or appearance. You want your child to understand that their parents look beyond shallow waters and understand them on a deeper and more sincere level. When you have cultivated a strong relationship with your daughter, her parents' opinions will be valued. As your child ages, she relies on your feedback and support, which is why parents have to be ready for whatever changes their child will choose to undergo because it should never waver their love for their child. As they enter into the teenage years, which are notorious for being difficult and rebellious, having a healthy and trusting parent-child relationship is crucial. These younger years are the years that set it up. Having a healthy relationship is not an easy feat, and it does not happen overnight because it takes much active effort for parents and children to have a strong bond.

For some parents who are still working towards developing a strong bond with their children, you may be wondering what a strong relationship looks like.

1. Listening: You should be able to listen to your child fully without judgment or interrupting them. Being a good listener and a confidant in your child's life is crucial because they will want to share what's going on in their lives with you without being prompted. Your job is to listen to your child and respect their choices. Likewise, your children also listen to you because they respect you and value your opinion.
2. Honesty: A strong bond features honesty about feelings from both parties where no one is downplaying their disappointment or anger. Being open and free with your point of view is

central to the success of a strong parent-child relationship.

3. Trust: Kids want to be taken seriously by their parents. When kids share their deepest darkest secrets with their parents, parents have to keep these secrets to themselves and avoid sharing them with people. It can be challenging for children to gather up the courage and be honest with their parents, but by doing so, they are indicating their trust for their father and mother.

4. Rationality: In stressful situations, your child might struggle to regulate their feelings in front of their parents. Rather than lashing out or responding with anger, parents need to temper their anger and understand that their child is having difficulty being rational. Stressful and emotional situations tend to cause children to lash out at the people closest to them, namely, their parents. And the same thing can be said vice versa, where parents will lash out at their kids. Understand that these words are fueled by anger. At some point in your childhood, you may have lashed out at your parents as well. Remember that no one is perfect, and children will say things that they don't mean. Having security in this will help you parent more confidently.

5. Boundaries: Some people mistake a solid parent-child bond with no limits because their child should be open and honest with every aspect of their lives. However, when it comes to a stable relationship, parents need to create the rules and accompanying consequences for proper behavior, which your child has to respect. Children always need guidance, especially during these younger years, and creating boundaries teaches them that while your parents can be your friends, they are first and foremost someone to respect.
6. Availability: The important thing is that parents will always make time for their child, even if it is simply 10 minutes of their busy schedule to chat with their child and to check up on their well-being. Always make time for your children. This is part of fortifying the strong bond that you have because your child will understand that you are constant in their lives, and you always will take the time to care for them.
7. Quality over quantity: Having quality one-on-one time with your child is the best strategy to show your child that they are valued in your life. Focus on the quality of interactions with each other rather than the quantity. New parents sometimes get nervous about

interacting with children because they believe that they need to entertain them excitingly constantly. However, understand that kids are just as happy talking to you when you take the time to be an active listener.

Chapter 6:
Ambition and Education

Raising Girls with ADHD

Girls with ADHD have trouble focusing. Hyperactivity and impulsive behavior tend to be more familiar with boys because girls experience less apparent symptoms. ADHD with girls tends to go unnoticed for many years because their signs are more subtle. Inattentive ADHD can manifest in the form of shyness and daydreaming. There is a wide range of how ADHD can manifest in a child, so parents must be proactive in observing their child's behavior at home and school.

Here are some signs that your girl may be struggling with ADHD:

- Inattentiveness: Within the classroom, if your child is easily distracted by a bird outside the window or spends her time daydreaming while teachers are talking, this can point towards ADHD. This is a fundamental symptom, but if you find the severity of her inattentiveness increasing, it may point towards something more serious, such as ADHD.
- Hyperactivity: This symptom is more commonly associated with boys; however, girls can also experience this. Hyperactive girls are generally dubbed as "tomboys" because they enjoy using their energy in sports or other physical activities. However, hyperactivity can also be seen through moving around in the classroom or having trouble sitting quietly for extended periods. This can also look like excessive fidgeting or wiggling in her seat.
- Impulse control: A lack of impulse control usually points towards ADHD. If your daughter is constantly interrupting others or speaking excessively, this can undoubtedly point towards ADHD.

It's important to remember that ADHD symptoms are not universal, nor are they linear. Every child is different, and many go undiagnosed for years. It is also important to remember that the people who have been diagnosed with ADHD can manage their symptoms and thrive in their lives, despite the circumstances. When it comes to raising a daughter with ADHD, the most important thing for her success is to work with her school and mentors to implement an effective intervention. Intervention can appear in the form of behavior management, medication, therapy, or counseling. This allows teachers to provide the academic services and accommodations that will help your daughter succeed. Having a proper diagnosis of ADHD can also help a child build their self-confidence because they explain why they may feel different compared to their classmates. Rather than letting them feel stupid or humiliated, your child will feel validated and understood.

For a child experiencing ADHD, they are sure to undergo some sort of personal and social struggle because they feel misunderstood by their peers and sometimes even the adults around them. The reality is that ADHD is a genuine disorder that many children suffer with. ADHD can seriously hinder an individual's emotional well-being and self-confidence, which reflects on their academic performance. Without intervention, this can seriously harm a child's development because they are experiencing tough challenges through their most crucial years without the support and guidance they need.

Chapter 7:
The Internet

In the age of screen, social media, and the Internet, parents are responsible for helping their kids safely navigate through the online world. Parents are constantly debating about screen time. A big issue that has arisen over the years is the fact that screens are the new babysitters. During these crucial ages between three and eleven years old, your child will quickly learn what technology is and how it serves as a form of entertainment and education. But as they age, the more sinister side of it can make itself known. For parents who are raising young girls in the Internet age, how do you manage the influence of social media on your daughter's life?

In recent years, YouTube has become a powerful platform for children. There are hours of content being churned out on the platform catered explicitly towards children within this demographic. While YouTube is an excellent resource for education, if parents are not careful with monitoring their children's content, their kids can quickly be exposed to mature content.

As mentioned several times throughout these guides, when it comes to parenting, kids always turn to their parents for guidance, which means that adults have to remember that they are examples of proper behavior. Parents must consciously force themselves to stop relying on their cell phones when they are around their children. Most adults would say that they spend too much time on their screens, translating to their children who see their parents rely heavily on social media for entertainment and distraction from the real world. This can encourage unhealthy behaviors and coping mechanisms, especially when faced with many different challenges in life. Especially when they are reaching their teenage years, kids are more likely to become victims of cyberbullying. They are also more likely to be focused on their smartphones and iPads than their academic work.

Social media seems to be the root cause of a lot of bullying in the past few years. Platforms like Instagram and Twitter, and more recently, TikTok, have become extremely popular among the younger generation.

Unfortunately, these applications also market themselves for children, when in fact, there is mature and adult content being shared on these platforms. Technology tends to give children too much access and exposure to mature themes, which can seriously affect how they think and how they may be perceived in school. In addition, these platforms do not continuously regulate against violence and drugs, which can be extremely dangerous for kids who are still in their developmental stages.

Interestingly, many parents find that because kids have been exposed to technology and social media, they seem to be more entitled because they have higher expectations and higher demands. Social media and influencers share lifestyles that are not necessarily the perspective of the average family yet prey on young, impressionable children. Social media also takes away from family time because your children would rather spend their time glued to their screen watching videos or playing games on their devices.

Another major issue for kids being given the technology at a young age is that they could be potentially exposed to online predators. As much as these apps have mechanisms in place that limit their screen time, technology is not impenetrable, and your child's privacy can be jeopardized when they are placed in front of a screen.

Additionally, another recent issue is internet addiction. Kids spend upwards of forty hours a week in front of screens when these hours could be spent exploring the world and having real-life experiences. When watching videos or playing games, it can be straightforward for kids to lose track of time or even go so far as to sacrifice crucial hours of sleep that are important for their development. Kids can grow irritable when they are not allowed to spend time online, and they may even forgo doing their homework or chores in favor of screen time. You may even begin to see disobedience because, despite your measures to set time limits for Internet usage, your child may be going out of their way to use their iPad or smartphones after hours when it is bedtime. In addition, it is prevalent for children to lie to their parents about the amount of time being spent online.

Parents tend to underestimate the capabilities of their children when they are given the iPad. Dangerous friendships can very quickly be formed online, especially when kids are the target. Internet addiction can also manifest through your child losing interest in their hobbies or extracurricular that were once passions. They may also be occupied with the thought of getting back to the Internet when they are away from it. Because the Internet serves as an escape for many children, this can have harmful effects on their mental health as they are still developing. Kids are sacrificing valuable sleep time to feel stimulated and excited by entertainment on the Internet. Children seek gratification and rewards from the online world and neglect their relationships, which is undoubtedly where the parent-child relationship can suffer. They may even develop social anxiety because they are not equipped with the right skills when faced with meeting people in the real world. They have been so preoccupied with spending their time online rather than developing genuine face-to-face relationships with other people.

When it comes to addressing your child's Internet addiction, there are a couple of strategies that can be employed to stop their behavior:

The first thing that is incredibly important is to address their problem. Your child may not see that what they're going through is a real problem unless you take the time to explain to them that they are experiencing the adverse effects of the Internet without even realizing it. Discuss the various instances that you have seen your child giving in to their addiction. Focus on developing goals to redirect their time and energy towards more productive things like hobbies or schoolwork. As a parent, you want to be mindful of your child's words when speaking to your child. Remember to allow them the chance to talk because it is more likely than not that you will have opposite opinions when it comes to this issue. Your child will not understand where you are coming from and may get incredibly emotional when they are told that they need to reduce their reliance on the Internet. This may result in outbursts or tantrums, but as a parent, you have to stand your ground and reiterate that while your child's feelings are valid, this is a meaningful conversation that you will need to be addressed before it is too late.

It's essential to be computer savvy yourself. Be sure to learn about monitoring software specifically made for parents and install the right filter so that your child is not exposed to mature content. However, despite the software that exists to keep children safe, things tend to slip through the cracks, and your child can be exposed to content that is not intended for them. Therefore you need to take an active role in the content that your child is consuming by being informed through Internet logs and having honest conversations with them. The software for parents is also not meant to control or spy on their child. It instead serves the purpose of protecting them from the dangers of the Internet by keeping them informed.

You want to set reasonable rules and boundaries. Your child is essentially going to have to be weaned off a bad habit. Banning them from the Internet can ultimately be seen as a punishment, which is not necessarily the message you are trying to convey. Rather than seeing you as someone with their best interests in mind, your child will instead internalize resentment and view you as an enemy and more likely to go behind your back. Instead, focus on creating attainable goals together and coming up with a compromise that both of you are happy with. This way, your child feels not only valued but has also agreed to the rules because they have had a part in making them. When your child does act up and breaks the rules, remind them that they had a role in creating the guidelines initially, which is why they have to continue to adhere to them.

Like many of her peers, Hannah was developing an Internet addiction. Every waking moment would be spent on her iPad, where she chatted with her friends and watched her favorite Disney shows. This became a huge problem when report cards came around, and Hannah's parents, James and Tanya, saw that she was doing poorly in arithmetic. After having a parent-teacher meeting, the parents realized that Hannah had neglected to hand in several assignments on time and had even flunked a few tests. They immediately identified the iPad as the culprit. While James and Tanya knew that the iPad was not inherently a bad thing for their child's development, allowing Hannah the independence to manage her own screen time had been a mistake. Hannah entirely took advantage of her parents' trust and would spend hours on her iPad, well past her bedtime. This led to her falling asleep on important test days and neglecting her studies. When it came to having an honest conversation with Hannah about her iPad use, she instantly became defensive and even threw a tantrum which both parents hadn't seen in years since their daughter had just turned 11 years old. However, they realized that this conversation had to happen. They explained to Hannah that she had fully taken advantage of her parents' trust in her to do the right thing, which was why her iPad was being confiscated until she could show them that she had learned to be more responsible with her time management. As a result, they ended up coming up with a plan to reduce Hannah's addiction by allocating one hour every day after school to spend on her iPad instead of the five or six hours that she had been spending previously. James and Tanya also set up a system where Hannah was also able to gain more screen time as a reward for doing well in her classes and doing her chores and homework on time. Not only was Hannah less irritable afterward, but she had also started doing well in arithmetic again. The fear of almost losing all her iPad screen time was such a fear of Hannah's that she immediately put her head down and got to work. She learned that her parents were disappointed in her but respected them because she wanted to make right her wrongs immediately by agreeing to compromise because she valued their opinion.

Chapter 8:
The Joy of Raising Daughters

Raising daughters is one of the most rewarding privileges in the world because daughters will teach you so much about yourself. As you embark on a journey of parenthood, remember to constantly reflect on yourself as you teach your daughter to find her place within society. Parents can quickly fall into the trap of being hypocritical or overly critical, leading to resentment or mistrust that can shake the foundations of a strong parent-child bond. When you instill the excellent qualities and values into your child, work just as hard to embody these qualities to show your daughter that it is entirely possible. It will also show her that it takes a lot of effort to be a good person, and people are always working towards evolving and growing every day so that they are better people than they were yesterday.

One of the most significant issues parents will have when raising their daughters is to instill a sense of self-assuredness and confidence. These qualities don't come easily, and it takes actively working towards these goals to make them a reality in your life. When you teach your children these qualities, be sure to emphasize the fact that these changes never happen overnight.

For Heidi, who was raising her daughter Bella, she quickly learned that she had to model that same behavior for her child to be a good person. Sometimes, this meant putting on a mask to show her child her confidence and self-assuredness, even when she did not always feel it. However, Heidi valued honesty above all else and was always honest to Bella about her anxiety and stress. While others looked down on Heidi for always being so open with her daughter, Bella valued her mother's confidence in her ability to understand that her mother was going through hard times with her employment and mental health. Other parents believed that Heidi treated Bella as her therapist because they were not used to seeing such a level of comfort and security in a mother-daughter relationship. However, this was not the case at all. For Heidi and Bella, being upfront about the state of their mental health was the key to keeping them both grounded and secure. This allowed for honestly to flourish between them, and Ginny was never afraid to share with her mother that she was also going through difficult times with her eating disorder. By being honest from the start, they were able to work through their problems together and not feel isolated.

Parents might feel like they have to put up a mask of perfection before their kids because they are treated as role models and mentor from the moment they have a child. However, remember that it is entirely acceptable for parents to be vulnerable to children. Showing your kids that you go through genuine and raw moments teaches them that life is not always going to be kind to you and that no matter what your age is, you are always going to be a work in progress. Growth is not limited to children only, and adults can always benefit from having a growth-oriented mindset.

This mentality can be applied to different situations. Simply showing your children that you are struggling with something in your life is an excellent way to show them that you are human too. Kids want to believe that their parents are perfect and have the answers to everything. When kids have this mindset, they automatically assume that their parents are invincible, which is never the case. Parents are a work in progress, just as much as their kids are. Many parents might even scorn this and feel differently, but the reality is that parents need time to change and evolve just as much as their kids do. While parents have more significant responsibilities and different priorities than their kids, adults and children alike will more often be a work in progress, so it is essential to be realistic and honest with your kids.

Stacey was a bright student that always strived to do her best in school. Her mother, however, had become worried about her because it seemed like the only thing Stacey was interested in was studying and possibly reading in her spare time.

To many parents, that might have been a dream come true for them, but she was still concerned about her daughter to Veronica. Veronica was a single parent, having divorced Stacey's father when she was just a toddler. She had never been remarried and never went into another relationship after the divorce, as she only had time to work and tend to her teen. Part of her wondered if Stacey had picked up Veronica's lack of social circle because she never saw her daughter hanging out with many friends or doing anything beyond studying and reading.

She decided that she needed to take things into her own hands, and that meant changing the way Stacey saw her mother interacting with those outside of their home. One day, Veronica decided to make it happen. Veronica walked into her daughter's bedroom, and Stacey was engrossed in a new novel. She barely even noticed when her mother walked in until Veronica made a slight noise. Stacey looked up. "Hey," then went back to reading. "Reading anything interesting?" Veronica asked.

Stacey shrugged. "Reading a new book that Mrs. Brewster introduced to us. It's pretty interesting."

Veronica, who knew much about what was going on with her daughter and school, knew that Mrs. Brewster was her English teacher. "That's nice." She hesitated before adding the latter part. "I will like you to come with me somewhere." Stacey looked up, obviously intrigued. "Where?" she asked. "I know a co-worker that has a daughter about your age. She invited us out for supper." Stacey groaned and started to make up a million excuses to explain why she couldn't go. Veronica had heard them all, including the fact that she had said many of them too. However, she wasn't going to let Stacey out of this one. It would do them both a bit of a good. "It will only be a couple of hours out of the night. You can come back and read again another time. Just do this for me. Will you?"

Being a single parent, they had a pretty good relationship, so Stacey agreed, even though she knew in her mind she didn't want to do it. If it were going to make her mom happy, then she would. They left and went to the restaurant where Mallory and Megan already were. The minute they got there, Veronica worried that maybe she had moved too fast for Stacey. Megan was bubbly, outgoing, and the opposite of her daughter. Fifteen minutes in, though after they all had ordered what to eat and drink, it seemed like Stacey and Megan were getting along well. It relieved Veronica, giving her less and less time to worry and more time to talk to Mallory.

The dinner went well, showing Veronica that it was good for both of them. They decided to set up another time to get together, and even Megan and Stacey were talking about hanging out together sometime after school. When they got in the car, Stacey turned to her mom. "Thank you. That was fun," she said.

Veronica smiled and had to agree. It didn't hurt her to get out there and do something for a change that didn't include work. She even looked forward to going out again. So as stated earlier, evaluate yourself and see if there are ways you can change to make things better on how your daughter interacts. If Stacey hadn't gone out to the restaurant, she would have still been stuck in her room instead of finding new friends to add to her social network.

Present interactions can determine the future for you, and you should never shy away from that. Stacey had the chance to branch out with her mother's support, which gave her the confidence to reach out to somebody new and make a new friend. Both mother and daughter took the time to put themselves in a unique situation to improve themselves.

Please leave a 1-click Review!

I would be incredibly thankful if you can take just 60 seconds to write a brief review on Amazon or the platform of purchase, even if it's just a few sentences!

Conclusion

Parents must have a growth mindset to succeed in raising strong and confident children. This mindset teaches us to evolve and better ourselves, thus encouraging parents to become better versions of themselves. Parenting begins with parents, who are role models and mentors to their children from the moment they are born. Daughters look to their fathers and mothers for guidance, and parents must remember that their young and impressionable children will always mimic their behavior. This is why parents have to be responsible and make sure that they are constantly developing their behaviors and habits so that their children will grow alongside them.

Rather than criticizing and berating your children for their bad behavior, always examine your behavior and how that may have contributed to your child's attitude. Often, children act out as a response to overwhelming emotions that they are having difficulty processing, which is where parents need to step in and provide them with the guidance they need.

The tips and recommendations from this book are only practical when they are led from a place of kindness and love. Appreciate your children and consistently convey your love for them by supporting the person they blossom into. Remember to stay persistent as you shape your daughter into the woman she is meant to be by listening to her and respecting her wants and needs. As you bring a child into this world, remember that the world is their oyster, and you should raise them to believe that so that they lead their lives without feeling confined or constricted no matter what.

Raising Boys in Today's Digital World:

Proven Positive Parenting Tips for Raising Respectful, Successful and Confident Boys

Introduction

Some have equated raising boys to a wedding cake. This may sound far-fetched, but the two share quite a bit in common in terms of their processes. During the wedding, all the guests enjoy a well-made cake as part of the wedding experience. The ingredients added to make a cake give it the height, body, and flavor, creating a final product that is enjoyable for all of its guests. Children, in that similar sense, are born with blank slates. Ingredients, in this case, constitute knowledge, practice, truths, discipline, and such. Parents must instill the proper guidance within their children to discover their gifts and potential and draw it out of them. To do so, parents have to raise their children responsibly. With all the necessary instruments, parents have to help their kids become well-rounded final products who will have a place in society.

For parents, raising children will be one of the most challenging yet rewarding gifts life offers. In a complicated world and riddled with pressures, how can parents raise their children to be self-assured, strong-willed individuals? The pressure on parents' shoulders is immense. Many parents find themselves struggling to navigate through the various challenges that life throws at them, especially when it comes to raising boys. There is, undoubtedly, a difference between raising sons and daughters. Society gives each gender a varying set of challenges that they must face, and for a parent, it becomes their responsibility to set their children up for success. So how can a parent prepare their child for the challenges life will throw at their children? Ultimately, a parent will not always be able to anticipate every detail of their child's life, nor will they always be around to hold their child's hand through every difficult moment. Additionally, humans are prone to making mistakes, and despite all your teachings, your children might still stumble and make the wrong choices. Ultimately, this is part of life and how humans evolve and grow both physically and personally.

The best strategy for a parent to employ is to instill good values, virtues, and a moral compass into your children from a young age. This might sound easier said than done, but parents have been doing so for generations. These ethics and values are what they will take with them throughout their childhood, teenagerhood, and adulthood. This will also become the values they instill in their children, raising wholesome children who are loved and nurtured from the beginning of their lives. Despite the trends that have come and gone in parenting, with many methods of going out of date and unpopular by modern standards, parents have been able to navigate raising their children into well-rounded individuals.

As a parent, raising your children can be anxiety-ridden among moments of joy, heartache, and excitement. The stressful aspect of child-rearing is that parents are on a time limit. There is only so much time allotted for parents to instill discipline and habits that their children will carry with them into adulthood. The childhood years are formative years where they will form their attitudes and truths. While an individual undergoes countless life experiences that will change them and change their behaviors, parents are responsible for bringing out the finished product within their children to have a place in society to make it a better place.

What are some of the challenges that parents might face when raising sons?

- Ignorance: The truth is that adults don't always have the answers. When faced with difficult decisions that will impact the people around them, adults might not always follow through with a rational or logical line of thinking. So when it comes to their children, as all of the pressures add up, certain decisions can pose as a roadblock

- Unavailability: This applies both in terms of physical availability but also emotionally. Kids need ample attention to be shaped and guided into the best versions of themselves. Still, sometimes parents tend to feel overwhelmed by the number of other responsibilities they have, resulting in them being unavailable during their child's development.

- Technology: Social media is becoming increasingly problematic for mental health and wellness, especially for young and impressionable minds. Parents often find themselves struggling to keep up with the times and all of the demands that are brought about through social media.

- Hands-off approach: Recent years have seen the rise in parents taking a more laissez-faire approach towards parenting their children. The problem with this is that children need the proper guidance and knowledge to be set on the right path during their formative years. By taking a more laid-back approach, boys will not learn the basic foundations within these most formative years between ages two to twelve years old. They will continue to make a mistake after mistake as they age without facing any consequences. This can escalate and snowball, where boys will not be able to differentiate between right and wrong by the time they reach teenagerhood.

Parenting is filled with highs and lows, and most parents will agree that raising children can be extremely emotional. While your children are certainly the focal point when it comes to raising them, parents tend to forget to take care of themselves too. Amid the chaos, parents neglect their own needs and mental health, which can have adverse effects on their children almost immediately.

Self-care strategies for parents
As a parent, you must make sure to take time for yourself. Between work, chores, picking up the kids, school events, family time, and the hundreds of other things you have to juggle on your plate and find the time to care for yourself. Children are incredibly aware of the emotion around them and will very quickly pick

up on anger, frustration, and negative energy, in general. While completely hiding your feelings from your children is an impossible feat, a more effective course of action would be to find at least thirty minutes to yourself every day. Try and make it a habit to find some peace to yourself that is uninterrupted. Whether it is right before bed or first thing in the morning before the chaos erupts, find some time to exercise, meditate, pursue a hobby, etc. Take the time to separate yourself from the chaos because it can seriously wear you down and make you irritable and short-tempered. It also allows you to clear your head and encourages a positive mindset when you are met with the day's challenges.

10 Self-Care Tips for Parents:
1. Meditate: A quick 10-minute breathing exercise first thing in the morning can set your day up for success. Inhale positivity and lightness, and exhale stress and tension.
2. Have a to-do list: While it may seem like having a to-do list is counterproductive to self-care for a parent, sometimes you can't avoid having hundreds of things to do during your day. Staying organized prevents you from getting too overwhelmed with the daily tasks of life.

3. Spend time outside: Enjoying nature can do wonders for your mental clarity. A quick walk around your area can get blood flow going and clear your mind. Experiencing fresh air and greenery can improve your mood drastically.
4. Listen to music: You don't need to set time aside to listen to music. Having some classical or inspirational music while you go through some tasks during your day can significantly boost your mood.
5. Join a book club: Carving some time out of your day to read is a great way to forget about life's daily stressors. Focus on a good book and if you have the time, join a book club to meet new people and engage in mentally stimulating discussions.
6. Maintain a social life: As much as your kids are your world, take the time to meet up with your friends and catch up occasionally. Hire a nanny, find a friend, or get the kids to an extracurricular activity for some well-deserved "me time." Having a life outside of parenthood is just as important as parenting itself.
7. Journaling: Keeping a journal is an excellent way to stay in tune with your thoughts. Allow yourself to pour all your ideas into your journal. Think of it like a purge, where you can get the negative out of your system.

8. Digital detox: Sometimes, our most prominent sources of stress lie in the online world. Put your phone away and take the time to enjoy your surroundings.
9. Exercise: A good workout can instantly make you feel more like yourself. Whether it is running or dancing, carve out the time to focus on just moving your body and nothing else.
10. Practice mindfulness: Everyone has different ways of practicing mindfulness, but the most important thing is to focus on the present moment rather than the hundreds of things you must do on your list. Focus on getting one thing done at a time and taking baby steps to prevent yourself from getting overwhelmed.

Always remember that there is no "one size fits all" approach to parenting. Neither is there a single method of parenting that can be applied to every child that will make all of your problems disappear. Instead, this book's approach is to encourage parents to foster a nurturing environment during every stage of their child's life, which means development for your child, but also yourself.

One of the main rules that this book encourages might even be controversial as parents tend to forget to focus on themselves. For the parent, you must evolve alongside your children. Growth as an adult is often overlooked because adults are seen as mature and believed to have undergone all of life's challenges. However, parenting poses a new set of challenges that adults must face. By becoming too strict or adopting a "helicopter parent" style, parents often fall into the trap of behaving like an authoritarian figure in their child's life. Or it may be the other way around, with parents that are far too relaxed and allow their children to navigate life individually, without any form of guidance from an adult. Both are extremes that can have adverse effects on your child and their mental health.

Evolution can be challenging to apply in practice, but the easiest way for a parent to come to terms with this is by understanding that they are also growing and learning every day. As a parent, you would not apply the same parenting techniques to a toddler when they have reached teenagerhood. As your children encounter new social interactions and mature from the new emotions that life throws at them, they will go through a period of emotional development that parents will need to grapple with. These changes are also positive if parents can bring guidance and calm during their chaos.

While every child is different, and certainly every boy, this book will provide the guidance you need to navigate through the biggest challenges of raising sons. While these tips and tricks cater to assisting you by raising sons, keep in mind that most of the ideas in this book are universally applicable, regardless of gender. The primary purpose of this guidebook is to help you nurture your child with the proper foundation and groundwork to become the best versions of themselves.

After reading this guide, please feel free to leave a review based on your findings and how valuable the guide was to you. I would be incredibly thankful if you could take 60 seconds to write a brief review on Amazon or the platform of purchase, even if it's just a few sentences!

Chapter 1:
Challenges of Raising Sons

What makes a boy?

Aside from the physical and biological aspects that separate genders, there are a few other differences between boys and girls that make parenting different for both. From the get-go, boys are subjected to a "boys will be boys" mentality. The phrase is often tossed around to justify poor behavior, and this phrase is encountered during childhood and well into adulthood. This mentality is incredibly dangerous because it encourages boys to act irresponsibly and project a lousy attitude throughout their lives. After all, such a justification exists to fall back on when there are real consequences at stake. So, while the rest of society might be encouraging your son to act a certain way because of the "boys will be boys" mentality, parents have to make sure that when they are raising their sons, they are responsible, respectable, and do not subscribe to such an idea.

The biggest problem with this mentality is that it encourages boys to exhibit aggressive behaviors. Boys are often going to be subjected to the idea that they must exhibit "macho" tendencies. This means showing their strength, which often manifests in the form of violence. For parents, it is essential to nip this idea in the bud from a young age because allowing such an idea to fester from teenagerhood into adulthood can lead to some hazardous behaviors that will need more significant intervention to fix. In addition to encouraging boys to exhibit behavior, this mentality also continues to perpetuate gender stereotypes. At some point in their lives, a child has heard phrases like "running like a girl" or "only boys are good at math." These gender stereotypes limit boys and girls alike, which can have huge effects on children who are so young, impressionable, and still trying to find their place in the world. This will have an immense impact on their sense of belonging in society and struggle to navigate their way by understanding their existence.

When we think about gender stereotypes, we do not often think about how they can impact a person both unconsciously and consciously. Take a moment to consider how internalized gender stereotypes might affect your child as a student and eventually as a working member of society. We can think about how internalized attitudes about gender can prevent students from reaching their full potential. For boys, this often manifests in pursuing careers or hobbies that are seen as manly. We can also see how these stereotypes reinforce these ideas that a specific gender is better at certain activities, with one of the most common stereotypes limiting boys to math, science, and sports in school. Ultimately these ideas are incredibly limiting because it confines boys to a particular set of rules that they have to adhere to, especially when it comes to behavior. If a boy exhibits any habits or attitudes that can be perceived as feminine in any way, this allows people to ostracize him and view him differently; when in reality, these rigid binaries ignore the true capabilities of human expression, which is complex and diverse.

One of the most common places where we experience this mentality is at school, particularly in bullying situations. First, the mentality is a way of justifying "natural tendencies" that boys seem to have towards violence and aggression. The phrase allows these harmful behaviors to persist and is another way for adults to avoid a severe intervention because it is constantly used as an excuse. As a parent, how do you grapple with such an idea ingrained in the way society functions? First, the best way is by knowing that you want your child to grow up in a world that allows them to express themselves fully.

These stereotypes encourage your children to limit themselves and their capabilities. But as a result, this continues to create boundaries for their personality, potential, and gifts. The first step in the right direction as a parent is to understand that your son does not have to fit himself within the societal mold of what a boy should be. Parents tend to be afraid to speak up in social situations, but this aspect of fighting gender norms is crucial to your child's development because it shows them that they should never be complacent.

Anna is a mother of two boys and for her, getting a call from her sons' school during the day was never a good sign. Someone was either sick or in serious trouble. And her instincts were not wrong. The school had called her one day to ask her to come down to the headteacher's office where her son Jason had gotten into an altercation. When she sat down with the headteacher, it became apparent that her son had been bullying another student. This news was shocking for Anna, who never even considered her son to be capable of belittling anyone. But the headteacher shared that while this issue had not escalated to a physical altercation, Jason had been taunting and teasing another student for their looks. Jason was the younger of her two sons, and luckily, this was not the first time in the headteacher's office. Her older son Ryan had been caught up with the wrong group of kids during his years in primary school, which meant a severe intervention from his school. With Ryan, it had been Anna's first experience with her child making the wrong choices. She was mortified, and her immediate instincts told her to become extremely defensive. In the end, Anna learned that Ryan had been in the wrong, and she needed to fix her attitude if she was going to help her children avoid going down the wrong path. So, when it came to Jason, Anna knew that she immediately needed to have a serious talk with her son as well as take away a few of his privileges because of the bad behavior. In addition to the lecture, Jason had to make amends with the classmate he had been bullying by writing an apology letter to him and his parents. Anna had been determined to make sure she was more proactive with Jason than she had been with Ryan, but she also knew that sometimes things fall through the cracks. As a parent, it is impossible to stay on top of everything your child does. But the most crucial part about the whole experience was that Anna evolved her parenting style to avoid becoming extremely defensive about her son and brushing off his bad behavior. Rather than sweeping his poor choices under the rug and making excuses for her son, she chose to face the problem straight on by having a serious discussion with Jason and turning it into a learning lesson for the two of them.

From Anna, we can see how she could take the lessons from her previous experiences and apply them. Whether you are having trouble in child-rearing with your first or fifth child, the biggest takeaway from Anna's experience is that she grew from her mistakes and continued to persevere. She took responsibility for her son's behavior while also making him accountable for his actions. While she was confronted by the school headteacher, rather than shutting down or getting defensive, she understood that her son had made a mistake, which reflected on her as well. Anna chose to speak up and point out her flaws and point out Jason's wrongdoings.

Parents are the first people to see the changes that their child is undergoing, which is why being more vocal about the fact that this creates a divide between girls and boys fosters the best environment for their children. Gender stereotypes can also foster unhealthy behaviors. When a child witnesses their parent speaking up against injustice and unfairness, this reaffirms the importance of constantly evolving and revisiting the way we treat our children. We know that phrases like "boys will be boys" are used to justified violent, degrading, and dangerous behavior, so addressing this from a young age and teaching your son that there are specific rules that we must follow to respect the people around us is incredibly important.

When we question what makes a boy, you will find that every answer differs. Every child is the product of their environment that their parents have fostered. Even twins are never exactly alike. And so, every child is going to be unique in their way. Attempting to fit your child into a specific mold will never yield good results because every child has their unique path that parents cannot interfere with. Instead, parents must help their children develop the means to reaching their full potential. Boys can be sensitive, emotional, gentle, and many other adjectives that are rarely associated with males. Instead of squashing any of these tendencies, it is the parents' responsibility to ensure that their sons are secure in their personalities and attitudes rather than shame them into embodying the "macho" stereotype.

Parenting in today's modern age is undoubtedly a departure from thirty years ago, especially when technology was not as accessible. Technology plays a massive role in our everyday lives, and when we consider how it might impact parenting, there are several benefits. For parents, the internet is an incredibly valuable resource because it has all of the answers to every question or concern. It is an excellent tool for parents who are seeking support and guidance from seasoned parents. Plenty of parenting forums exist for this sole purpose. Technology is also great for children. Not only is it a resource, but it also works as an educational tool and can create social connections from all around the world, thus expanding your son's worldview without having to travel anywhere. Thirty years ago, entertainment was undoubtedly more limited, and education was confined to the classroom. Nowadays, kids can explore any topic using the internet and educate themselves without an instructor's need. For parents, this is a revelation as it opens up an endless world of possibilities for your children.

Your Free Gift!

As a way of saying thank you for Your purchase, I have included a gift that you can download at TCEC publishing .com

Chapter 2:
Core Values

By the age of 12, children should be aware of the realities in the world and be equipped with the core values that will guide them for the rest of their lives. Parents might assume that the easiest way to do so is by approaching core values methodically and strategically. However, the most logical way to instill the correct values into your child is simply by embodying them yourself. In short, a parent must practice what they preach.

Core values are ultimately up to the parent to decide, but the main points are universal for both girls and boys alike. These are important for a boy's mental and physical upbringing because they are the foundations of a well-rounded boy. Before we delve into a boy's interests and how to nurture them, the first step is to instill these core values into them so that they understand that they have a responsibility of their own to be an upstanding member of society who contributes to the world to make it a better place. These core values shape your son to develop an adaptable mentality and implement positive thinking rather than negative.

10 Core Values to Teach Your Child

1. Respect: Having respect for peers, classmates, parents, relatives, and even strangers is crucial. Instilling this in your children from a young age will teach them that everyone deserves to be treated like a human being and should be regarded without prejudice or bias. This is crucial from the classroom until they become independent members of society. Kids will constantly be faced with conflicting world views and differing experiences from their own. Teach them that diversity exists, and we should be respectful of other experiences because this is part of growing up.

2. Honesty: This is a big one for parents, especially. As your child navigates through their life, they will be sure to make plenty of mistakes that they might even be ashamed to tell you about. While you can say to your children that lying is wrong, the better way to

instill honesty within your child is by embodying it. Parents should avoid lying and possess a truthful disposition. Additionally, teach your children the differences between honesty and being polite. Children have the tendency to lie. Parents must be observant of their children, especially when they are younger, as they are still pushing the envelope and testing the boundaries.

One parent recently shared a story where her son Michael was usually quick to complain when she sent him on an errand. For example, when Michael's mum would ask him to do the dishes or clean up his toys that were left out, he would always grumble and complain. However, every time Michael was asked to accompany his Mum to the corner shop to run errands and carry the shopping in, he was very eager to do so. He was extremely helpful to his Mum when they went to the corner shop, which was surprising because he always voiced his unhappiness with everything else. One day, Michael's mother noticed that he was stealing sweets and chocolates by slipping them into his pocket when he thought no one was watching. She was horrified because she couldn't believe where he could have possibly picked up such a bad habit. She finally realized why he was always so eager to run these errands with him. Michael was caught, and she had a long and serious conversation with him about it, lecturing him about honesty and why it was incredibly wrong to steal. Michael apologized to her and the corner shop owner, which was humiliating but necessary to teach him his lesson. His mother also told him to pay back the corner shop owner for all of the sweets and chocolates he had stolen, making a dent in his savings. It was a bitter pill to swallow for both Michael and his mum, but he is now 11 years old, and Michael's mother reports that he has not stolen anything since. The vital part of their success was that Michael's mother intervened early on and explained why it was wrong. Some of Michael's schoolmates, who introduced stealing to him, continue to do so because they have not been taught this behavior is unacceptable. It can lead to more significant consequences as they age.

3. Accountability: Earlier in the chapter, we shared the story of Anna and how she chose to take responsibility for her parenting which had relaxed briefly, thus allowing her son to act poorly. She embodied this response in front of

her son, which encouraged him to take accountability for his poor actions. Boys will constantly be given a pass throughout their lives. Please don't allow this to happen by teaching your children about responsibility and giving them consequences when they mess up. Not only does this teach them that there are boundaries in society, but it also instills in them a sense of righteousness by understanding that they should not be given a pass just because they are male.

4. Empathy: Children are still navigating through the different emotions that they are experiencing. They are incredibly perceptive to the emotionality around them, but they may not always know how to react appropriately. Teaching them to be kind to those experiencing differently around them might seem difficult to conceptualize at first. The best way to do so is by guiding them through emotions and attempting to frame how your child might feel during a particular situation. This will get them to think about how they might be affected by a specific emotion, thus enabling them to understand what someone else is going through. It can seem challenging to form guidance, but talking through experiences is an excellent way to start.

Sometimes, children act in a way that is seemingly out of character that you begin to wonder what they were thinking and why they do what they do. There might even come the point where you question if you even knew them as well as you thought you did. One instance of this was when a young boy named David played ball in the garden while his little sister, Jessica, played with her doll. When Jessica got in Michael's way, Michael became incredibly angry and frustrated. In his rage, he cruelly threw the toy away. Michael and Jessica's mother rushed to the garden when she heard Jessica's cry. While their mother was frustrated with the situation, she chose not to show it because it would have been counter-productive to teaching Michael how to handle his anger and frustration. Remember that children are always looking to their parents for guidance, so is it so important for parents to model the proper behavior.

The conversation below ensued:

Mother: Why did you throw her doll away, Michael?

David: She got in my way, mum. I was playing my ball.

Mother: Do you know your sister liked that doll?

David: Yes, mum.

Mother: Do you like your ball?

David: Yes, mum.

Mother: Would you like me to throw your ball over the garden just like you did to Ellen's doll?

David: No, mum. I am sorry.

Mother: Would sorry change anything?

David: No, mum.

Mother: So what did you learn?

David: Never hurt people with what they value.

Mother: Plus, whatever you do to anyone would be done back to you by someone else, got that?

David: Yes, mum.

And that's it. Let children know that whatever they do to anyone would be done back to them. They ought to treat people the way they would want to be treated. This is an essential lesson to instill in children and growing teenagers to help them maintain good relationships as they continue to grow.

5. Patience: Life can hit you quickly, but certain moments can happen at a snail's pace. Your kids might be used to having everything within a moment's notice, but many things in life might not occur at the same pace. Prepare them for this by teaching them to wait.

Patience is often a virtue, and expecting something to happen in a heartbeat is simply unrealistic. Acknowledge that there is difficulty in waiting. While we might be used to instant gratification, it is important to instill that this will not always be the case.

At this early stage in their lives, boys are generally guided by self-interest, where their feelings and emotion tend to cloud the little judgment they have developed. They are driven by immediate gratification and don't quite have the foresight yet to consider the consequences of their actions. They are ready to cross any border and push the envelope because what they see now is the only thing that matters.

For Mrs. Alli, teaching her son patience during his birthday was a challenge. He desperately wanted to open his gifts during his party, like all his other friends did, but Mrs. Alli forbade him from doing so until after his party. But it was simply the polite thing to do, as they had guests to entertain during their party. While her son wanted to play with his new toys, Mrs. Alli had to insist on putting it off for another few hours. It was incredibly frustrating for him, but his mum decided that this was a chance for him to learn the virtues of patience early in his life to be ingrained in him as he aged and faced more unexpected situations that tested his patience. As much as he wanted to have what his friends had, he persevered his mum's discipline. Established values are like a guiding light that leads a child's way through life. Boys who have values regard it above their life. Boys without values lack a moral spine and standards of living that will hold them firm through life's upheavals; so, wherever the wind blows is where the tide takes them.

It's much better to guide your son towards developing patience in their personality than to have them focus on the instant gratification of wanting stuff.

6. Determination: Determination can go a long way, especially when paired with ambition. Teaching your child that there will always be highs and extreme lows in life is a way to set them up for success. Part of the journey is picking yourself up when you have hit your lowest of lows in life, which can hit anyone at any time in life.

At the age of twelve, Isaiah was struggling with mathematics in school. His marks were poor, and he was very disinterested in the subject, choosing to spend his time instead of playing football with his friends. Maria sat down with her son and devised a plan to work on his mathematics exercises over the summer holidays to be prepared in time for the next school year. She struck a deal with him; if he passed his mathematics exam with good marks, she would allow him to play for their local football club. With the right motivation, the results were almost instantaneous. Isaiah was determined as he followed Maria's plan, studying a chapter of mathematics every week. However, Isaiah still despised mathematics, and there were many moments of frustration because he simply did not understand the concepts. When this happened, Maria would change her teaching approach so that he would understand better. He did marginally better during his first test of the school year, but his marks still were not good enough. Isaiah was frustrated, irritable, and angry because all of his efforts did not pay off. Maria took this opportunity to instill determination in him by teaching him that success did not magically occur overnight. Especially in low moments like this, he had to pick himself up and keep going. Maria continued her drills with him every week, and eventually, he passed his mathematics exam with a good enough grade that allowed him to play football. Interestingly, the lesson about determination followed him as he played sports. He applied the same philosophy during challenging and disappointing moments when he was playing football.

To form the proper personality in your son, raise the child in a program or schedule, a routine to guide the child intentionally to discover the personality you aim. Each day, aim to do something with the child. It may not be more than 20 minutes every day, but choose a topic to teach to achieve the core values of the personality they should become. Take them through the periods of value formation. "Many studies on personality distinguish three types: resilience, over controllers, and under controllers. This typology is based on the theory of ego-control and ego-resiliency by Block and Block". Whether your child is a 'resilient' or an 'under controller,' help them understand who they are, take pride in it, and flourish. It will do them a world of good when it comes to their overall attitude, positivity, and determination, giving them every chance to accept who they are and go on to succeed.

From ages five to twelve years old, you may want to spend, say, an hour drilling into their minds systematic instructions so that by age fourteen, they know where they are, e.g., how not to fall under pressure, how to overcome trials and conflicts... This is systematic parenting and nurturing. If you don't have a systematic way of training your child, what will happen is that the baby will be fed, have fun, go to school, do all those expected things, but nothing is constructed within. The child is just growing in the body, and the inside is not increasing. The consequence of that is that no anchor is provided to hold and secure the child in times of emotional crises. The child is empty in the core; he is not anchored, and lacks any direction in life, and would not know what to do at the right time.

A child with just a body and a name is like windblown away. He is empty because he does not have an internal structure or spine to hold him up in the time of crises. He is like a ship without a compass, nothing to navigate him from inside. Such a child will be living only for himself, without a direction for proper neighborliness with others in society. Children must have the inner mechanism for stability in life; else, they might stumble and fall. But they will be able to stand because of the internal balance of their value-based personality.

If a child has values, he will rule over his emotion; he sees himself as having his life as a means to accomplish the purpose for which he was created. Life is about purpose. A kid's life and personality are to be equipped for purposeful living. Life must be intentional for a goal. A kid's purpose and intent in life must be stocked for them from when they are small. "Children thrive when they have secure, positive relationships with adults who are knowledgeable about how to support their development and learning." Please do everything you can to show them the way for purposeful living. They will grow up to thank you, and in later life, likely use the same techniques you used on them but with their children.

7. Curiosity: Having an interest in exploring the diversity and uniqueness in the world can propel your child to find their passions and leave a mark on society. Instill curiosity by encouraging them to ask questions about their environment. Read books, watch different programs, and explore the world outside. Curiosity can lead to a lot of untapped

potentials, especially when it is practiced throughout life.

8. Justice: Instilling a sense of righteousness can seem like a massive feat to try and teach your children. But from a young age, showing them the realities of the world through the racism that exists is one way to expose them to injustices that many people of their own age experience. Teach them to make amends and apologize to right their wrongs. This ties in with accountability and being responsible for their actions, especially when they hurt other people.

9. Courage: Life is going to throw extreme emotions in your child's way. As much as you want to be there always to protect them, your child must come to terms with their individuality. There will be plenty of situations in life that will require your child to take a plunge and be courageous. A strategy parents often use is by exposing their children to different extracurricular activities. It offers them the opportunity to face new dynamics and social situations, with an element of a unique experience like a sport or a skill.

10. Love: This one seems like a no-brainer, but showering your children with love will teach them to be generous with their emotions, especially for sons who are told to avoid being

emotional. If parents are open with their affection daily, this opens up communication between parents and children and allows them to express their appreciation outwardly.

These ten core values are the cardinal rules that are crucial to having a well-rounded child. These are also valuable ideas that cannot be instilled overnight and will take time and repeated practice for your children to understand their importance. As adults, we are still flawed and continue to make mistakes. Just like our children, we are constantly working towards becoming the best versions of ourselves. Teach your children to follow through with these ideas in their everyday lives, which is possibly the most significant challenge for a parent as you cannot constantly watch their every move.

For one parent named Michael, his experiences in parenting have revealed more about himself than he initially had anticipated. Michael had recently been laid off, which was the cause of a lot of anger and strife within his household as he was bitter over unfairly losing his job. He spent an increased amount of time at home and caught his son using bad language and neglecting his schoolwork, which was shocking and certainly not something he anticipated. As Michael and his wife Jenna looked for the source of their son's poor behavior, Michael came to realize that he was essentially looking at a mirror image of himself in his son and not in a good way. Michael had been lashing out at his family members over the loss of his job and had become entirely unmotivated when it came to looking for new employment. He had spiraled into a depression, which inadvertently played a role in his son's development. For Michael, he found that his bad mood was hanging over his family like a dark cloud, and after some prompting from Jenna, he ended up going to therapy to resolve some of the issues that had been swept under the rug. While the changes did not occur overnight, Michael and Jenna's son's behavior seemed to get worse before it got better. Michael ultimately realized how his attitude played a prominent role in dictating his son's behavior. From his perspective, fatherhood forced him to look at himself and how he carried himself around his family because his son was at an age where he was highly impressionable. Not only did he have to practice accountability consciously, but he also had to model the behaviors that he wanted his son to reflect.

Bearing these core values in mind, we can delve into a boy's physicality and mental state. In terms of the physical condition, this aspect is essential for your son to develop interests that teach them new skills and improve the existing skills. There are so many learning styles that exist, and when your child discovers the area they thrive in, this can be applied to interests where they will flourish. The learning styles that exist are auditory, visual, and tactile. Auditory learners study through hearing and listening. They can remember things and store information more effectively through spoken lectures and reading out loud. Visual learners succeed by relying on imagery such as flashcards and drawings to retain concepts. Tactile learners use a hands-on approach and find that physical activity helps them understand better. Many students are a combination of the three. Understanding how your son learns can be the building blocks to a plan to pursue some interests in line with their strengths. This can be accomplished through various hobbies, sports, and activities. These activities that involve the physicality of a child will benefit him in many ways because it allows him to express himself and build self-esteem, which inevitably ties in with his mental state. Taking up an activity or hobby as a growing child teaches children to set and achieve goals, problem solves, and make decisions for themselves, translating into a sense of individuality and independence. This is also an excellent way to instill a sense of productivity within your son's lives. While relaxing is important, spending the time to work towards their goals is equally as important and should be prioritized.

When we tap into the mentality of children, creating a stable environment for their upbringing is crucial. Children should be comfortable and have a consistent lifestyle so that they can function at their highest potential. Mental health can be complex to delve into because as children mature and experience new social connections, they are also susceptible to developing anxiety and depression. For a long time, children's mental health has gone ignored because children tend to be quite resilient in the face of hardship. While this is true in many cases, mental health must be prioritized as much as physical health. If a child were to get seriously injured, the immediate response would be to take them to the hospital to get medical treatment. In that same way, mental health should be prioritized and treated seriously, especially if children undergo some severe changes in their lives. While they may not be confident enough to share what they are going through, they will feel encouraged to do so when they see that their mental health is just as important.

Chapter 3:
Raising Sons as a Single Parent

Father figures, particularly for sons, play a crucial role in their development. Kids do well when their fathers are personally engaged with them. When fathers take an active role in their son's life, this opens communication and encourages transparency and honesty because sons may find themselves able to relate to their fathers more than their mothers. Of course, this can differ wildly depending on the individual's circumstances, but fathers are crucial in the mental well-being of their sons. Because men are stereotypically seen to be less affectionate than mothers, some fathers tend to struggle to provide their son's support.

So what exactly does an engaged and active father look like? These tips are specifically geared to sons, who often don't experience involved parents because girls are often regarded as more emotional, requiring more emotional support. But the reality is that sons have the same emotional capacity and are often at risk of dealing with mental health issues because they don't experience enough emotionality as they grow up. Because kids cannot fully express the extent of their emotions with their parents, they end up bottling them for years, festering resentment and anger that can manifest in unhealthy ways. Or, in many other cases, when children grow up to have their own families, the cycle continues, and many issues continue to go unaddressed. The generational cycle continues as boys grow into adulthood and become fathers themselves, maintaining the same taboo around their feelings. To break the cycle, fathers must be doubly proactive when it comes to developing a relationship with their sons that is not only honest but also comfortable.

- Quality over quantity: Take the time to make memories with your child. Rather than counting the minutes, you spend with them, think about the unique memories you can share that will draw you closer. Quality time is precious, especially for children. Some parents might find this difficult, but quality does not mean elaborate or expensive. Take the time out of your day to show up for important events like school performances, games, etc. Know your child's schedule and make it a point to show up to express your care and appreciation for them.

- Acknowledge their individuality: Remember that your children are human beings who have unique personalities, so take the time to get to know them and learn about every facet that makes them who they are.

- Be honest: One of the core values of parenting is being honest and open with your children. Share the emotional complexities that you are experiencing with your kids. This does not mean lay all of your problems with them but show your children that you are not all-knowing and immune to emotionality and extreme feelings. This allows them to see that their parents are human, just like they are. Doing so encourages them to open up and share their struggles.

- Avoid judgment: For any parent in any situation, judging your child as they open up to you is one of the sure-fire ways to get them to shut down and keep things from you. As much as you play the role of a parent and bear the weight of responsibilities, sometimes your child is simply looking for someone to talk to. While your immediate instinct might be to lecture them and attempt to offer a solution, they may not always be looking for that.

- Be present: Take the time to listen to your kids truly. It can be easy to fall into the role of telling your child what to do and constantly nagging. Remember that they are developing, and their thoughts are growing increasingly complex as they mature and face new situations. Listen to their thoughts and feelings and be a reliable shoulder that they can lean on, especially when they want to get things off their chest.

The reality of the world is that families look different everywhere. Some children might not have father figures in their lives, and mothers might have to juggle both roles and wear different hats as they guide their children. The next chapter delves into the unique pressures and challenges that boys face. But for mothers who have the stress of having to play a father figure as well as fulfilling the role of being a mother, this is a unique challenge that can be extremely difficult to navigate as it is another added responsibility on top of the hundreds of other things that parents must fulfill. It can be extremely overwhelming, and frequently, parents feel like they are doing too much and too little at the same time without making any progress. Being a single parent is incredibly complex because raising children is traditionally seen as a two-person job. Mothers might find themselves caught in a difficult position when raising sons as single parents because they cannot immediately relate to their sons as a father figure would. However, it is essential to remember that all kids are extremely different. For single parents looking to foster the most nurturing environments for their sons, here are a few tips explicitly catered for you:

1. Create a routine: Having structure in your life is an excellent way to prevent life from getting too overwhelming. This is also a perfect way to spot any anomalies in your children, whether it's a change in behavior or emotion. This also organizes your life so that you can classify all the essential things.
2. Cope with your guilt: At some point, parents will feel guilty for spending time away from their kids. Find a healthy way to deal with your guilt because it is inevitable that you will have to leave your kids, whether at school or with a babysitter.
3. Build a community: Having friends or other family members to lean on is an excellent way to reassure that you are not alone. They are also great babysitters in case of emergencies.

"It takes a village to raise a child" is a famous African proverb that parents have heard at least once or twice. But it holds merit because as much as you try to do things on your own as a single parent, there is no shame in relying on the people around you for support.

4. Be honest: Being honest with your child can be a slippery slope, but expressing your emotions and showing them that you are having a hard time will teach them some of life's hardest lessons about empathy. Be sure to keep how much you share with them age-appropriate because kids cannot fill the role of being your therapist.

5. Remember to lead with love: As you juggle the number of things you need to do during your day, remember to shower your kids with love, affection, admiration, and praise. Because this is a no-brainer, we can often forget its importance and leave it on the back burner as daily life stressors continue to pile up. But prioritizing this is not only suitable for your child but also reminds you to slow down and take a moment to breathe.

6. Help them build relationships: While single parents do it all, sometimes they can't fulfill every need that your child may have, especially when it comes to navigating through

inevitable challenges that life presents. Sometimes, while you can extend sympathy and offer comfort as a single mother, you might not have all the solutions. Help your child connect with their teachers, coaches, and other role models so that they have more than one reliable person to lean on. Helping your son build a community will enable them to feel secure within themselves and have the confidence and courage to venture out of their comfort zone because they have a village supporting them.

7. Be a guide: Remember that kids are constantly absorbing your attitude and behavior. Children will look to you as their role model from the minute they can differentiate between the people in their lives. As they age, they will meet plenty of new faces who will ultimately have some sort of impact on their lives. Part of parenting is accepting that you won't always be your child's immediate source for guidance, but that does not mean that you will also ever relinquish your role as a guide to your children. As a guide to your kids, remember always to model the behavior that you expect your child to exhibit. Set a standard for conduct that applies to both children and adults.

Bear in mind that boys today face a unique set of pressures and challenges that mothers might not be equipped to meet. However, mothers can still extend their empathy and love towards their sons to become reliable comfort and guidance sources.

Michael and Michelle's Family.

When Michael and Michelle got married, they resolved to get to know each other as much as possible and sort out their differences before having kids. All their married friends had warned them that having children would be unlike anything they had ever done, and they truly did not understand what they meant until they were in a house full of three kids.

They were parents to three children named Luke, Mark, and Florence. Michael was sterner between the two parents and taught the boys to respect and obey him. When the boys were much younger, the boys feared their father because he often played "bad cop" compared to their mother, the "good cop." Michael was militant in his discipline and instilled important values like patience and respect by not tolerating any lousy behavior met with consequences like an early bedtime, no playtime, or no dessert. Their friends often marveled at how polite and well-behaved their children were. As they aged and learned the boundaries and rules that their father had, their fear lessened because they were always on their best behavior around their Dad. The reality was that they learned to act up only when Mum was around. Their mum was far less strict than their dad because Michelle often left disciplining them up to Michael. Their children were aware of this dynamic between the two parents and often took advantage of this, even from a very young age.

Mark and Luke do get on well with each other, but being so close in age meant that the two often started fights and roughhousing. Mark often provoked his brother by burping loudly at the dinner table. In response, Luke began poking his brother in the arm to get back at him. The two continued for a while, and they began to make a mess of the dinner table as they roughhoused each other.

When the playing became too much, Mark complained to his mum, exasperated, and only wanted a peaceful dinner. "Why did you provoke him by burping in his face?" she asked, frustrated at how the boys were fighting again. Mark could only shrug. She turned to Luke, who complained about his dinner being ruined, "Well, you shouldn't have annoyed your brother! You've both made a mess of the table!" Their dinner was strewn all over the table, which was now another mess that Michelle had to clean up.

Michael took this exact moment to come home from work. All he could hear from the front door was shouting and yelling between the brothers and his wife. "Stop it, Mark and Luke! This behavior is unacceptable!" he shouted, and the chaos instantly died down.

Michael stepped in, ordering the kids to apologize to their mother and making them clean up the colossal mess they had made. Michael knew that his wife did not like disciplining their children because she felt terrible when punished. As their father, he deliberately took the role of disciplining their children so that they knew to respect their mother no matter what.

One of Michael's friends named Alli would often come to their house after dinner to enjoy a drink with Michael. He, in contrast to Michael, often disrespected his wife and was constantly rude to her. Alli's kids were aware of how their father treated their mum because he never concealed how he spoke to her around them and would constantly get upset and angry at her in front of them.

Michael was also aware of the way Alli treated his wife and told him that the reason why his marriage had lasted for so long through all the challenges of parenting was that Michael and Michelle took the time to get to know each other as much as possible before their kids were born. They knew the minute their kids were born, and they were sensitive to their emotions, including anger and strife between parents. Couples who don't overcome this and bring resentment and unhappiness into their marriage will negatively affect their children with the same emotions. During their first three years of marriage, Michael and Michelle even went for marriage counseling/therapy together to create a clear plan of how they wanted to treat each other and their kids. While some parents often judged Michael and Michelle because disciplining their children was solely left for Michael, this was an agreement that they had come to before they had kids. The two of them learned to get all their anger out of the way and control their speech respectfully and patiently. They knew that disagreements were going to be inevitable during their marriage. Still, they learned techniques to cope with each other and sort out their differences without hurting each other's feelings and being negative, which would have impacted their children's development, especially when it came to how they would treat the people around them in situations that challenged them.

As a friend and father, Michael implored Alli to show his children that he had to honor his wife so that they would reflect the respect that she deserved. Alli had to control his speech around his wife and speak kindly to her without being cruel or disrespectful. He explained to Alli that while his marriage was never perfect, they led by example and modeled the behavior that their sons would copy, setting an example for their younger sister Florence.

These values that were instilled in their children would follow them as they aged and became adults. When their children went to college, they reflected the values of their households. They carried themselves well because Michelle had drilled the proper values into each of them from infancy to teenagerhood. They took advantage of their most formative years between the ages of two to twelve years old and trained them to be well-behaved and respectful to people. For Michelle, while disciplining was not the area that she focused on with their children, she was more so focused on how to instill the correct values and bring them up to be the best versions of themselves, and this was what Michael and Michelle had agreed upon prior to them having children.

Within Alli, he left all the childrearing to his wife, Joanne. Their son Liam and daughter were entirely her responsibility because Alli's interests lay in making money as a businessman. For Joanne, Michelle became a role model for her because she looked to her for parenting tips. She had to single-handedly raise her son and daughter because Alli was not interested in getting involved. She was able to train her son to develop the right attitude and behaviors. She was also responsible for disciplining her son so that he was on the right path. Joanne was so successful in raising Liam with the help of Michelle's advice that Liam was chosen to become a role model for other students in his school and head prefect for his leadership capabilities.

For Mums reading this, you can do it just like Joanne. If you have a husband who is not contributing to raising your child, you can do it yourself with courage and strength. The time parents have with their children is short, so take advantage of the time you do have with them. It is a woman who builds the house, not the man. Ultimately, the wisdom of a woman builds the whole atmosphere of the house. Women are so much more capable than they might believe themselves to be, and sometimes they simply need a bit of encouragement to take the leap and raise their children with or without a partner around for various reasons. For Joanne, having a support system like Michelle was crucial for her to take charge of her motherhood and raise Liam to become the best version of himself, despite the hostile atmosphere at home between his parents.

Chapter 4:
Mentoring Boys

How do we go about mentoring boys so that they reach their highest potential? One of the first steps to take is to give your child as many opportunities as possible to explore different avenues for self-expression and creativity. Some children find that they thrive in a creative environment and enjoy the arts through music or dance. Others may find that they enjoy sports and strategic thinking in a teamwork setting even more. There are so many opportunities catered towards helping kids find their passions in life from a young age. As a parent, these teachers introduced into your son's life serve as another mentor figure in their life who can guide them through their passions. They have the technical and practical knowledge that a parent may not always have when pursuing a passion like music or a sport.

Whatever the activity that your child chooses, it should allow room for your child to learn, grow, and improve constantly. Having a skill that is continuously a work in progress encourages core values like determination and curiosity, which should be established from a young age so that kids can carry these values with them into the various stages of their lives. The activity should give your child opportunities to make mistakes and go beyond their comfort zone to be challenged constantly.

Remember to respect their interests. The previous chapter looked at the stereotypes that follow boys throughout their lives. While it can be tempting to push your child into "manlier" extracurriculars like sports, this might not be what they want. Societal pressures shape the way we think, and sometimes, these biases can rear their ugly head when we least expect them. Parents might feel pressured to conform to societal standards out of fear of their child being seen as strange or weird. There is certainly a stigma surrounding boys pursuing arts, for example. However, the challenge here is for parents to combat these inherent biases and have confidence in their son's abilities. Limiting them only prevents them from reaching their full potential.

Once your son has established what he is interested in, applying the list of core values towards his interests is an excellent way to nurture an environment that celebrates his achievements and encourages him to feel secure in his choices. Especially if your children express their interest in a particular activity, take advantage of this by providing the resources they need to improve their skills and evolve. Sometimes this can end up becoming a career path that they will pursue later in life. And for many others, it can end up being one of their hobbies that they are passionate about.

Megan's son Travis had enjoyed playing with Legos and toy planes when he was younger. Megan noticed that he enjoyed building different things like buildings and machines. He enjoyed the tactile aspect of Legos and applying logic to the various pieces to make something complex. While these toys are undoubtedly familiar with young children, Travis had taken such a liking to them and expressed that these were his favorite toys at a young age. Megan jumped at the opportunity and bought several toys and games all about planes. It became clear that she had made the right choice because she noticed that Travis only ever fixated on these particular toys. As Travis aged, he eventually grew out of these toys, but Megan noticed that some of the skills he had developed from his toys were being applied in his new interests. One of the afterschool extracurricular activities that he ended up pursuing was robotics, where he created robots alongside his peers. He was using the same tactical and logical skills that he had developed as a child. Travis found an interest in mechanical engineering in primary and high school and ended up pursuing aeronautical engineering when he went to college. While not all toys point towards a child's future career path, you could reach potential when you focus on your child's interests. Megan had exposed her son to several different toys before discovering that he loved playing with Legos and toy airplanes. Another essential element to Travis's success was that he was surrounded by people who encouraged him to be brave and pursue the unknown. His robotics club instructor served as a mentor in his life and pushed him to try new things in engineering, which was something Megan did not have the knowledge to do. Allow other role models to come into your child's life so that they develop strong connections and further their skills and knowledge.

Mentorships are unique because they are designed to help the student broaden their horizons within a specific field. For kids, mentors can come in the form of teachers, coaches, and role models. For boys, the realm of mentorship can be difficult to maneuver because it might seem intimidating. Many boys also avoid seeking help because of gender stereotypes that look down on males who look for guidance. But childhood consists of some of the most formative years, and having the right mentors can guide your son down the right path. Having a role model, especially a successful male figure, can inspire and encourage your son to be ambitious, dream big and fulfill his purpose and passion.

What does a successful mentorship look like for your son?

- Commitment: From both mentor and mentee, having a meaningful connection is vital. When both parties regularly show up with a positive attitude, this is the key to education and a beneficial relationship.
- Realistic goal setting: When a mentor understands their mentee's goals, realistic aims can be achieved. But a mentor should also know how to push your son to think outside of the box and aim higher than they anticipated. For example, for Travis, his coach encouraged him to pursue engineering in college when he did not believe he could do so and even provided a letter of recommendation to attest to his skills and knowledge. Having a mentor who encourages you to go beyond what you think you can (while also knowing your limits) is essential to the relationship.

- Engagement: Have fun and share experiences to develop a positive relationship. Not only is your son's mentor a reliable and trustworthy source in their life, but he also provides the support that they need. Mentors should help boys develop socially and emotionally by listening and observing your son. They should do so without judgment. Your son has to find trustworthiness and reliability to feel comfortable sharing all of their thoughts without a filter. As a parent, it is vital to make sure that mentors are professional and reliable before subjecting your son to them.

- Empower your son: As a parent, you want to see your son thrive no matter what. While your son develops a close relationship with their mentor, please encourage them to commit to new opportunities fully. Be another source of support for your son that a mentor cannot by providing emotional support and comfort whenever they may need it.

- Avoid comparisons: Your son is a unique individual, and you want to support this fully, yet parents sometimes feel inclined to compare their kids with others. Respect the fact that your child is different. Avoid putting the pressure on what other kids are doing with their lives onto your son because it will only demotivate him.

- Be fearless: Allow your son to explore the different avenues that arise from mentorship and committing to their interests. This will allow him to have a deeper understanding of his interests, passions, and he might even find another related field that he might want to pursue. Inspire your son to be fearless through the journey of mentorship because finding the right mentor does not happen for everyone.

- Recognize wins and losses: As his mentor guides your son, you should acknowledge his accomplishments. Recognition often contributes to boys and a teen's self-worth, and while it is nice to be appreciated and recognized by an adult, make it clear that these achievements are not his sole purpose in life. These achievements should be building him up rather than bringing him down when he does not meet his goals.

While mentors can shape and mold your child, the household is where all of these critical skills begin to develop. Many boys do not have access to mentors for several reasons, so it becomes the parents' responsibility solely to develop these skills. Alongside the core values that you should be instilling in your son, there is also the added responsibility of providing a firm yet loving guidance that boys need. Parents might struggle with raising motivated, cooperative, and confident boys, so here are some simple strategies to get you started.

How to provide the guidance your son needs within the household:
The following skills often come up within the household. Working on them takes a little bit of practice, but by setting boundaries with your sons early on, they will grow to learn and adopt these practices so that they carry them well into adulthood. Honing on these skills makes for a well-rounded person and prepares them for the world outside, which can be brutal and unforgiving.

Self-reliance: One of the initial habits you should try and instill in your son is a sense of independence. Having the confidence to rely on themselves is vital, especially as they age and enter the professional sphere, which can sometimes feel lonely as they are in a new environment. When your son is a child, start by teaching him simple skills like cooking and cleaning up after himself. This teaches him that not everything will simply be handed to him, especially regarding his everyday lifestyle. Encouraging him to take care of himself when he can is an excellent way to build the needed skills that lead up to independence as he ages. Having the responsibility of a few household chores can help your child develop a sense of duty and require them to work on their time management skills.

Mrs. Kate shared a story about her experience with her friend's son named Alex. Mrs. Kate was at the shopping mall one day and saw Alex. She immediately noticed how uncharacteristically quiet he was being. She used to drive Alex and her son to swimming lessons, and he was usually very cheerful and lively. Today, however, Mrs. Kate noticed that he shrank away from her when she greeted him. She was immediately aware that something was not right. A woman she had never met approached her and introduced herself as Alex's guardian. Confused, Mrs. Kate asked where Alex's mother was. Alex's guardian explained that his mother had tragically died of COVID-19, and Alex had since then been living with her. Mrs. Kate was devastated, but she also realized that Alex was in good hands. He had been well-prepared by his mother with a good moral compass and strong virtues. Despite being nine years old, Mrs. Kate knew firsthand that Alex was polite and respectful, and he was always looking out for her son, which made him a good friend. Alex had undergone a tragedy at such a young age but was mature beyond his years because his mother had instilled the correct values in him.

Common sense: There is book smart, and then there is street smart. Teaching your son basic survival skills outside of the home isn't clueless, especially when you are not around. Start at a young age by allowing him to make simple choices. Avoid doing everything for him. Instead, allow him to experiment or explore so that he can have the confidence to make decisions as he gets older. This doesn't mean that you should entirely relinquish your parenting role. Guide him down the right path while also giving him the chance to choose right from wrong. This can sound like extra work when it is easier to do things for him when he is younger. But the reality is that kids are more intelligent than we think, and they need an opportunity to show this.

Concentration: Concentration is like a muscle that needs to be exercised throughout your child's life. Especially when kids are young, they grow increasingly accustomed to technology that entertains them for hours on end. Teaching your son to sit quietly might be one of the more difficult tasks because kids love moving around, being noisy, and are just learning boundaries. Encourage your son to spend some time on quiet activities like drawing, coloring, or reading. These activities are great for mental concentration and work on your son's creativity and imagination skills. They have to entertain themselves, rather than rely on the TV or video games. Set a reasonable time for quiet activity and slowly build on that until they eventually pursue it independently.

Impulse control: Kids who don't understand their emotions are more likely to be impulsive. When it comes to your sons, make sure to call them out on unacceptable behaviors. You should model the behaviour that you expect your children to embody within the household. Parents are the immediate role models that sons have, so be conscious about responding to certain situations that illicit intense and emotional responses. There is nothing wrong with getting angry, but your answer is crucial to show your sons how to react appropriately.

Combating aggression: With boys, aggression is a serious topic that often goes unaddressed. If you see your son exhibiting aggression that you do not like, it is crucial to talk to him about it instead of leaving it to fester. Try and figure out what triggered your child's aggressive behavior. Understanding where his frustrations come from can help develop the right strategies so that he does not react aggressively the next time something similar happens. Teach him to redirect his anger and respond calmly when something does not go his way or is frustrated. Rather than taking it out violently, teach him to take a moment to breathe and assess the situation.

Disrespect: Set clear rules within your household for what is tolerated and what is not. Your son should be able to differentiate between acceptable behavior. While he is bound to make mistakes, let him know that inevitable mistakes can have consequences. Learning takes time, so be patient. But be sure to be observant whenever your son exhibits poor behavior and responds accurately. When disrespect is not addressed early on, this can manifest later on in life, especially when your son has his own family and has to deal with many different types of people throughout his professional life.

Academic success: Your son must understand from a young age that their academic success is their responsibility. Good grades get rewarded and are essential for the trajectory of their life. From elementary school, high school, and college, your son will always be evaluated, so aiming to do his best is essential. Remember that it is okay to make mistakes and even fail. Parents often forget that their sons are so much more than their grades, so if your son does not do well, try understanding why rather than scolding them for doing poorly. Kids are learning and might not always understand the importance of school. The critical aspect to always encourage is that your son must pick himself up and keep trying until he succeeds.

As you get to know your son and learn from him, several topics are essential to broach as you guide your son throughout life. Some of these topics may be uncomfortable to discuss, but they are crucial to have an open discussion about avoiding these topics' stigma. Forget about your awkwardness when talking about these topics and focus on the fact that they are vital for your son to be informed. Establishing that you are open to talk about these things will encourage your son to be more open about his struggles.

1. Mental health: Talk to your son about how he is doing mentally. Many boys and teens are susceptible to depression and anxiety, so give mental health the importance it deserves. Because boys are encouraged to bottle up their feelings, avoid this taboo by having open conversations about their emotions. By discussing it more frequently, it becomes the norm between you and your child to share what they are experiencing regarding their mental wellbeing.
2. Gender identity: As your sons are maturing, they are learning more about themselves and

their identity. As a parent, you must listen to them to understand them.

3. Internet safety: The internet and social media have become an integral part of our everyday lives. Educate your children about the dangers that lie on the internet and how to be safe. For boys approaching the ages 10 to 12, they are usually being exposed to the internet around this time. They might know more than you about the internet. Reiterating that the internet is a dangerous place never hurts. Remind him to be alert and never share private and personal information. Practice safe habits when using social media and always protect himself when putting his image out there on the web.

4. Saying 'no': Boys need to understand the power of 'no' as much as girls do. The word 'no' sets clear boundaries and can even protect lives. Boys are often overlooked when it comes to dangerous situations because of stereotypes, but never assume that your son is completely safe. Prepare him for uncomfortable situations and offer him solutions for how to get out of them.

5. Racism: Make sure that your son is educated on discrimination worldwide and educate him on unacceptable language that is still often heard. Racism exists in most societies, so

educating your son on this topic also teaches him never to participate and tolerate discrimination of any kind.

These topics might seem uncomfortable for many parents to discuss with their sons, but part of the process of raising well-rounded sons who are prepared for the world is by removing the stigma around such conversations. These conversations are essential to have because they protect your son and teach him boundaries and rules about the personal space in society. As you develop your relationship with your son while he matures, have serious conversations about important topics to show him that the world is not always a fair and justified place. Instill a sense of righteousness within him by having these conversations. This will motivate him to combat the injustice that continues to plague societies around the world.

Think about how you learn as an individual and how they tie in with your current hobbies and interests. Consider the path that has led to you taking up your current hobby and how the activity itself has shaped and changed you both in terms of physicality and mentality. When you consider your hobby, factor in the different skills you have to bring to the table. Think about the social connections you might have made when pursuing this hobby.

Chapter 5:
How raising boys differ from girls

Boys are often not seen as emotional, whereas girls are. While this is a vast generalization, this usually starts when boys are not given enough affection and love as they are growing up. Everyone carries baggage with them, whether it is trauma from their childhood or a previous relationship. For parents, it can be easy to bring the same unresolved trauma into their childrearing habits, which can make it extremely difficult for their children to thrive. For mothers and fathers alike, wounds must be healed so that they can raise their sons without the added baggage that creates limitations and fear.

As you navigate your way through teaching sons the value of hard work and being a working member of the community, all of this can be threatened if a parent's previous trauma mingles with the values that they are attempting to instill within their children. For the mother and son dynamic, this can be especially difficult. Mothers might have unresolved issues with men like their own fathers, brothers, or previous relationships. When it comes to strengthening her relationship with her son, this might require added effort because of the mental and emotional exercise it might become. For mothers looking to strengthen or even rebuild a relationship with their son, here are some tips that can be applied to your parenting.

During the kindergarten years, girls seem to be better at reading feelings and forming relationships, while boys appear to have a greater understanding of spatial relationships. Girls improve their verbal skills faster than boys, according to research. On the other hand, young boys appear to use words less, favoring noise and sounds like car-engine sounds and imitating animals.

There are differences in raising boys and girls in the playground, where the gender divide is most visible among school-aged children. Boys' games are frequently focused on winning. Boys like to play in large, organized groups where they can keep score and work together and rival one another. Girls, on the other hand, prefer to play in small groups of two to four people.

They enjoy having discussions and sharing ideas, emphasizing teamwork and support.

While there are discrepancies between boys and girls, parenting leaves a lasting mark on children – especially when parenting boys and girls according to gender stereotypes. For example, some mothers tend to avoid being overly affectionate with their son for fear of them turning into a "mama's boy." This can mean if they were to hurt themselves, a mother might avoid rushing to comfort him. When playing with other kids, if a son is exhibiting more violent tendencies as he roughhouses, a parent might be more lenient simply because he is a boy.

So how can mothers find the balance to raise extraordinary sons? Ultimately, it is by providing encouragement, education, and practical advice. Parents have the responsibility of equipping their sons with the tools they need to succeed in life. Some parents, especially mothers, tend to focus on the external upbringing of their sons. This can have the adverse effect of leaving them unsecured because they are unprepared to face the hardship life brings. They cannot face the world and the extreme changes that will occur as they age into their teens and beyond.

Here are some strategies for mothers to develop a deeper connection with their sons:

Learn to speak his language: Boys bond through activities and competition, so find out what your son loves to do and consider taking the time to experience his favorite activity with him. For example, if your son loves tennis, learn the basics, and join him for a game. Perhaps your son is interested in learning more about one of your interests. Whether it is cooking, painting, or dancing, find common ground with your son and use that as the foundation to spend time together.

Accept every part of him: You might not be able to completely relate to your son and his masculine ways because men and women tend to be quite different. However, these differences are what makes the relationship unique. It might be challenging to relate to your son at first but develop a connection with your son by getting to know him and accepting all of the parts that make him who he is.

Teach him what you know: There are probably a few things that you are pretty good at, and this might even be something he admires about you. Taking the time to share your expertise with your son is an excellent way to bond with him. Not only does he learn from you, but he also gets a chance to spend the time developing a skill with you. One everyday activity that leads to a strong mother and son relationship is cooking. Show him the ropes around the kitchen and teach him a valuable skill that he can take with him well into adulthood.

Embrace a growth mindset: A common trope in parenting is when parents feel the pressure to be perfect. As a mother, being open and honest about your mistakes and moments where you have messed up reinforces the idea that you are just as human as he is. This will encourage him to share his struggles and help him grow to understand you as well. Because humans are so susceptible to mistakes, encouraging a "growth mindset" rather than a "fixed" one teaches your son to take the lessons from his mistakes and apply them to his life to evolve as an individual constantly. Rather than focusing on the fact that he messed up and was wrong, focus on the circumstances surrounding the mistake. Identify the "why" and have an open discussion about where exactly he went wrong and why they made such choices. In the future, your son will have a better understanding of how to respond appropriately.

One-on-one time: Take the time to talk to your son one-on-one. It can be easy to forget to spend time together, especially throughout the chaos of daily life. While these moments are part of the daily routine, taking the effort to allocate a particular time for you and your son to relax and talk casually can make it feel much more special. As a mother, it is in your nature to want to know everything that your son is going through, but sometimes it is essential to know when to stay out of it.

Pick your battles: Your son will go through some rebellious stages in his life, especially if he is between ten to twelve years old or approaching his teenage years. Teenage boys are generally very stubborn and opinionated. This is usually when parents find that they are getting into the most arguments with their sons. As they are maturing and figuring out their place in the world, they also learn more and form their own opinions. Do your best to avoid getting into enormous fights. Some battles are just not worth it. Try to encourage discussions and respectful conversations to voice different opinions without getting into heated yelling matches.

Do your homework: Remember that all relationships take work. If you are trying to build something from the ground up or strengthen your relationship with your son, remember that a good parent-child relationship takes time and effort from both parties to improve. It takes time to develop the trust that is the foundation of all relationships, and it certainly does not happen overnight, as much as you might want it to. Persevering and showing your son that you want to support him and be there for him is how he will see that he needs to make an effort.

Take the time to nurture: Children are often equated to plants that need to be nurtured, watered, and given the right amount of sunlight to thrive and grow. Sometimes, despite all of your efforts, your plant might still wilt, even though you are doing everything correctly. Your plant might need fertilizer or extra watering to perk up again. The key here is that it will need extra care to get back into its shape. Rather than criticizing your plant or giving up on it, you take the time and effort to restore it.

Similarly, as your son grows up, he is going to undergo plenty of changes. He will be experiencing new things and encountering new perspectives that will change his worldview. Rather than criticizing him for the changes that he is undergoing, take the time to correct him kindly when he is wrong and give him the benefit of the doubt. Criticizing him will only shame him and stunt his evolution as a person.

Forgiveness is critical: Don't take things too personally. Your son or teenager might be at that stage where they constantly argue and seem always to want to pick a fight with you. While this behavior is certainly not acceptable, he can also potentially say something that might hurt your feelings. As much as it hurts, this is part of the sacrifice that is parenthood. Try not to take things too personally as your son is completely tangled up in their feelings and having difficulty expressing themselves in a level-headed way. Teenagerhood is a time where they will be immature, and they will struggle to find the right words to express their emotions. Parents are bound to be in the line of fire, and your children will say something that can hurt your feelings. Remember to forgive your kids and take the time to teach them that taking out their anger on you is not a suitable coping mechanism. Show them the proper way to handle emotions. Try to remember what it was like when you were a kid and how you might have overreacted when you were young and immature.

Try having a discussion: Resisting the impulse to want to punish your child for making mistakes constantly. Once upon a time, especially in the olden days, the punishment was often the response to everything when it came to parenting. A mistake that was made was immediately met with drastic consequences or privileges being taken away. Nowadays, there is a lot of merit in having an adult conversation with your son when acting up or making poor decisions. Kids need a lot of guidance, and simply punishing them will not teach them anything. Instead, constant punishment will only threaten the foundations of your relationship with him and will encourage him to lie and hide things from you.

Spirituality for Sons

For different families, spirituality plays an active role in shaping the family. One of the main ways parents can nurture their son emotionally is by helping him develop a spiritual connection when he is younger. Raising a spiritual child can seem quite daunting at first because spirituality is incredibly personal. Children might not grasp the extent of a higher power because it can be complex to explain. But just like most things with parenting, kids learn from behavior that is modeled before them. Parents want to instill a sense of morality and ethics, and one of the effective ways to do so is by instilling a sense of spirituality. But how do parents get their children to believe in God? How can parents explain the complexity of spirituality to their sons? Having a strong sense of emotionality is the first step to opening the conversation about spirituality. Getting your child to talk about their feelings openly and without fear of judgment gives them the confidence they need to share ideas. In return, they will be open to new ideas and concepts that involve spirituality and God.

Especially when it comes to raising boys, emotionality is never discussed enough. There is such a stigma around boys discussing their true feelings and revealing how hurt they may have felt over certain situations because the expectation is for boys to brush things off and move on simply. On the other hand, girls are seen as more emotional and therefore allowed to linger on any wrongdoings and negative feelings. This thinking is dangerous because it will enable boys to shut away from their true feelings and encourage them to bottle everything up. No matter what kind of trauma a child is dealing with, the worst way to handle this, especially as a parent, is by ignoring their triggers and allowing them to shut down or bottle up their feelings completely. But if a child were undergoing some mental difficulty, laying the foundation from the start to deal with these issues head-on opens your son to be more in tune with his feelings and emotions.

If your child undergoes some trauma, while he does deserve some alone time to think about how this has affected him, it is just as equally important for a parent to intervene and try and guide him to heal correctly after giving him the chance to process. While you allow your son the emotionality within the household, he might not be given the same opportunity in a public setting. As you hold yourself to a higher standard and give your son the chance to explore emotions, a teacher, for example, might not give him the same opportunity to do so, which is why it is so essential for the household to be a safe space for your child.

As you get your son to be comfortable sharing his emotions, this leads into other avenues that he will want to share with you, such as his hopes and dreams. It is important to nurture his hopes and ambitions in life. But a bonus is by having the element of spirituality intertwined within that, which can boost his morale and let him know that he always has someone to lean on, especially when the road to his dreams is particularly challenging. Knowing that God is a constant force of comfort and guidance can be exceptionally comforting for someone experiencing the trials and tribulations of life. As your son goes through life, meets new people, changes his environment, makes new choices, and implements different ideas into his life, knowing that God is always going to be there will serve as a constant reminder that he is not only loved but also being protected by a higher power.

Once you have established with your son that it is okay to be open with his emotions, the next step is to teach him mindfulness methods. An excellent way to incorporate this regularly is by looking for spirituality in the environment that surrounds your son. Look for concrete ways where you can talk about how God's presence is omnipotent. Involve your son to have faith and engage him by making prayers part of your everyday life. Whether it is just another day or something unique, get your kids involved, explain why you pray, celebrate specific dates, and explain why you might have particular practices and how they tie in with spirituality. Be open with your spirituality with your child. Explain to them why you feel a certain way about your beliefs and how God has shaped your life and changed your life for the better. Show them how God can be a positive force in their lives and boost their confidence and self-esteem as they navigate through the challenges of life. How you live and incorporate God into your everyday life is an excellent example for your children to follow and even take inspiration from. Your son will likely have a lot of questions about spirituality and how it fits into the everyday world, and this is your chance to show them concrete examples about how God fits in your life and how you involve God in your daily life. For example, if you pray, it would be so beneficial to pray together as a family. Prayer can also extend into discussions about how your son's day has involved God in any way. Being open with each other is one of the joys of spirituality itself. This will be different for every person involved in various religions, but ultimately, leading by example is one of the main ways to share your spirituality with your sons.

Another effective way to get your child involved with spirituality, especially if he shows the first signs of interest but not entirely clear on how to navigate through his beliefs, is by involving him in community activities. Community centers often have activities or festivals that are geared specifically for children and teens. These serve the purpose of teaching students to understand the structural components of spirituality while also developing a deeper understanding and connection with other members of the community. Another way community centers often do this is by connecting kids with volunteer efforts. Charity is usually a significant component of most religions like Christianity. This might take shape in the form of visiting a nursing home, perhaps spending time with senior citizens, or even volunteering for a soup kitchen. These different activities can make some lasting memories for your son that translate into their appreciation for their spirituality. It also teaches them valuable lessons about good deeds and charity.

But it is also important to remember that we should never use spirituality to manipulate children and teenagers into doing what we want. Spirituality is incredibly personal and the backbone of an individual. Using God to force children to do things or change them by saying, "God won't love you because you are bad" is incredibly harmful and dangerous. This can destroy a very sacred relationship between an individual and their God. So while there are going to be so many moments where your son will test your limits and push your buttons, it is never a good way to handle things by using God against them.

James wanted to incorporate spirituality into his son Tom's life but found it awkward and uncomfortable to try and broach the subject with his son. Eventually, with the support of his wife, James brought up the topic during dinner one evening. Initially, Tom was not actively participating in the conversation, choosing to listen instead. After a little bit of gentle prompting from James about Tom's thoughts, the conversation began to flow, and James and Tom found that they shared a lot more in common about their views on faith in God than they had initially expected. While the family had always celebrated Easter and Christmas and occasionally went to church, they never quite found the time to discuss their faith and the role it played in their everyday lives. By opening a casual conversation, James got to know his son a lot better and drew connections between them, which ended up bringing them much closer. James found that he could have deep conversations with his son. He began to implement some of the strategies mentioned above to nurture Tom both emotionally and spiritually as he matured. Parenting plays a significant role in shaping spirituality because it allows boys like Tom to be open and forward about their faith before their family. The latter are some of the closest people to them.

Try having a conversation with your son or daughter today about what God means to them and gauge how they feel about their spirituality.

Kate and Andrew are parents to twin boys named Jack and James. Every Sunday, the family attended church. The boys were very involved in their local church community. They attended Bible classes for children, discussed the Bible, and participated in activities like singing and praying. Stephen, their teacher, was a young graduate full of life and shared the Bible engagingly and energetically. He was a favorite teacher because he was enthusiastic about connecting with his students and sharing the Bible in an illustrative way. Teachers play such a crucial role in shaping young boys because they allow boys to discover their interest and enthusiasm as teachers reflect the same attitude towards a subject. Jack and James saw Stephen as a role model for how he regarded the Bible, which was encouraging for Kate and Andrew. For homework, Stephen encouraged his students to memorize verses from the scriptures, which Jack and James were very eager to do every week before their Bible study class. This helped the boys garner a deeper understanding of God and apply it at home. Stephen also allocated quiet time during Bible study, which allowed students to jot down their daily findings from the verses they read and how they have applied these lessons into their lives. Part of the exercise included Stephen checking over the work and grading the boys on their thoughts and reflections from their readings. Stephen also encouraged a collaborative environment by allowing the older students to help the younger and less experienced students with their reflections. He also included a sticker system in his classes, where good work was rewarded with stickers, which greatly motivated the students. Bible study has influenced Jack and James in their everyday lives by encouraging them to pray with the rest of their family in the mornings before the start of their day and at night before they all go to sleep. This practice continuously helped the boys maintain their connection with God on their own.

Stephen invited the boys over for their eighth birthday, and while Jack and James were in his house, the boys saw Stephen's mum and grandmother praying over their food together. This was a new sight for Jack and James, but Stephen explained to his students why his mother and grandmother did so – which greatly inspired the boys to start doing the same within their own home. They continued this practice as they grew up and applied the same principles to everything else in their lives.

Chapter 6:
A Hard Hill to Climb

As much as this book aims to avoid using gender stereotypes, in this case, raising sons, it isn't a secret that boys are very rambunctious and enjoy being loud and playful. More often than not, they are more active than girls. For parents who are raising young boys, things can get extremely stressful and overwhelming very quickly. Boys tend to be more energetic and physical than girls are and enjoy roughhousing and playing aggressively. At the same time, there are, of course, exceptions; parenting sons will always take up a lot of your time and effort. Many parents feel like they are at wit's end because their sons are almost too much for them to handle. Despite the strategies that have been mentioned in this book, many parents might simply say, "What if my son just doesn't listen?" Some parents are really at the end of their rope because even with all of their efforts to nurture and guide their sons, they simply do not want to adhere to any form of authority and refuse to cooperate. There will be so many challenging days, and more than once, parents will feel like they want to give up.

Boys are more likely to be hyperactive and tend to be diagnosed with ADHD more often than girls. Many parents learn of their child's traits and immediately brush them off as "boys being boys," but these "traits" could be symptoms of something more concerning, like ADHD. ADHD is not just about being hyper, and it does not only affect boys. But because boys tend to move around and playing more actively constantly, the two tend to blend, making it doubly challenging for parents to discern if their child has ADHD or not.

How does ADHD manifest in young boys?
ADHD manifests in the form of hyperactive behavior that can also be impulsive. It can be challenging to differentiate between a boy who is being active and a boy with ADHD. Having a child who has ADHD can be extremely tough on parents because your son might receive a lot of negative feedback from the people they are surrounded by. For example, at school, your son might be labeled as "disruptive." This can seriously affect your son's self-confidence and self-esteem,

leading to disciplinary problems because they don't know how to cope with such negative feelings.

A common danger with children who go undiagnosed in classrooms is a cycle of anger and negative feelings. When a child with ADHD gets in trouble at school for being disruptive, he might harbor those feelings from getting in trouble at school and end up fighting with a sibling. The cycle of anger simply doesn't stop because he isn't being taught the right coping methods. His ADHD is being written off as "bad behavior" when he is having trouble being ignored. Dealing with the different dynamics within a household can exhaust parents and make them feel like they are unable to catch a break because their family is always in chaos. When you throw a child with undiagnosed ADHD into the mix, it might seem like an added challenge because your son is constantly moving around and needs to be simulated in a way that keeps him busy. Quietness seems impossible in a household like this and continues to wear down parents, causing their mental health and well-being to suffer.

However, all hope is not lost if you suspect that your child has ADHD. Kids with ADHD simply learn differently and have a unique way of thinking. The challenge for boys who have ADHD will be to make friends and fit in. With the proper guidance from parents and teachers, your son can overcome these social challenges. Every child experiences ADHD differently, and most children discover a positive outlet to express themselves. For example, music is a standard outlet for many young people with ADHD. If you are concerned that your child might have ADHD, there are several diagnostics available for them. There are also several treatments available for kids who are struggling with ADHD. Some kids respond best to medication, while others thrive with a treatment plan. Working with a mental health professional can help your son navigate the challenges and have someone to rely on who completely understands what they are experiencing. Professionals will also offer effective strategies that your son can employ in their everyday lives to cope with the stressors and triggers that might affect their ADHD.

There is a range of therapies that are available for children with ADHD, depending on their cases. Some kids require behavior therapy, while other kids might require cognitive behavioral therapy. Plenty of children find that they thrive on non-medication treatment options such as exercise, dietary changes, and meditating on scriptures. The efficacy of these treatments depends on your son and what his needs are. This can be determined with the help of your doctor. There are so many classroom accommodations that can be arranged to help your son with ADHD when it comes to schooling. Having the support of your child's teacher is one of the best ways to get started with creating an effective plan that will help your son thrive with his ADHD. As a parent, it is your responsibility to learn everything you possibly can about ADHD so that you can understand the extent of what your son is going through. Your child might even be experiencing anxiety or depression that ties with their ADHD. The more you know, the more you can help them with the people who can support and provide the accommodations for your son and create the best environment for him to thrive in.

One of the success stories involved a student named Christian who was in the first grade. Christian's homeroom teacher, Ms. Peters, noticed that he was having a lot of trouble in school. He was constantly being disruptive and refused to do any of his homework. Ms. Peters was growing increasingly concerned because he would fail his reading and math classes in his first grade of elementary school. It was incredibly rare for any student to flunk a grade in elementary school. Still, Christian rarely handed in his homework and was constantly interrupting class with his antics, which earned him detentions and demerit points. When he came home, Christian continued to lash out at his family and his mother Mariah was at wit's end about what to do. She had tried almost everything; she had taken away his video games and other privileges, and she had tried hiring a tutor to help with his poor grades. But Christian was incredibly restless and unable to focus during the tutoring sessions. Everything changed when Christian's homeroom teacher reached out to Mariah and shared her suspicions about Christian possibly exhibiting signs of ADHD. Mariah jumped at the opportunity to try and figure out why exactly her son was seemingly so disinterested in his education.

After a few evaluations with professionals and a long conversation with his doctor, Mariah discovered that Christian had dyslexia. He also had ADHD. His dyslexia had gone unnoticed for so many years, and he had managed to get through all of his previous years of schooling with the help of his homeroom teachers. Now that he was in the fifth grade and was expected to be more independent with his schoolwork, Christian struggled to cope with his dyslexia and ADHD but was not quite sure how to express his frustrations. Eventually, after the diagnosis, Mariah and Ms. Peters worked together to curate a workable and realistic education plan for Christian. They found that he really thrived with music, and so they devised out a way to incorporate music into his education and curriculum so that he had the opportunity to focus on the skills that were his strengths.

Additionally, Mariah and Ms. Peters worked together to figure out a few accommodations, especially for tests and his homework, so that he would have a chance to put his best foot forward. It took a couple of months of negotiations between Christian, Ms. Peters, Mariah, and the school board as they worked their way through trying to find the best course of action for Christian's education. Eventually, they figured out the best methods that worked for him after a lot of trial and error. Christian returned to doing his homework regularly and was enjoying school again. He was even making new social connections that he would never have pursued before. The takeaway here is that it took Ms. Peters noticing that Christian was exhibiting the symptoms of ADHD and taking the initiative to share it with his parent so that they could follow through with the right course of action. It was a long process that was stressful and overwhelming at times, but in the end, it was the right choice because Christian is back on the path to success and thriving in a way he never had before.

The truth is that parenting is a long battle that will take more time and effort than anything else you will ever do in your lifetime. There will be high moments that will bring you joy and pride that you would never have felt otherwise, and you will also experience some of the lowest lows. Parenting does not come easy for most parents, and they find themselves in for a rude awakening as they see their child grow up, change, and develop into the different stages of their lives. Having the proper knowledge and strategies behind your parenting can help shape your son into the best version of himself. However, it is always easier said than done. Even if you are equipped with all the tips and tricks, the only way you will improve and learn is by experiencing it firsthand. For first-time parents reading guidebooks such as this one, you will not understand the extent of the hardship and sacrifice it takes to raise children until experiencing it firsthand.

Even if your son is not dealing with ADHD, it is good to keep track of how he responds to different social situations. Building a relationship with his teacher to understand how he is doing when he is at school is an excellent way to see how your child is coping with all the other developments that can sometimes feel like they are coming so quickly that they might not even have a chance to process these changes correctly. While you can't always be informed of every single aspect of your child, you can certainly be aware of how they are doing in their day-to-day life when you are not around them.

One crucial aspect to keep track of is their aggression. For boys, it can be easy to play aggressively and not consider the ramifications of how their play might be affecting their peers or siblings. As your child engages with other kids and learns to play and interact with them, they may not immediately understand acceptable boundaries. Rough and tumble are very common for young boys, even into their teenage years. Parents might feel uncomfortable when they watch their sons interact with other kids because it might seem a little bit too aggressive. Video games tend to feature violent themes with weapons and fighting. While this does not mean that your child is inherently violent, it can undoubtedly lead to your child wanting to recreate the themes of their video games, movies, and TV shows in real life. Pretend play can sometimes involve some aggression taken too far if your kids don't understand how to respect other people's personal space.

With girls, sensitivity is something that they are familiarized with from a very young age. But for boys, the same cannot be said. Some parents might even say that developing their son's sensitive side takes a little more effort because they aren't used to tapping into this side of them as it can be so frowned upon by societal standards. As a parent, explain the importance of kindness and treating other people gently. An excellent way to do this is also by referencing famous men who exhibited both strength and sensitivity. You want to share with your son that he can have different facets and that boys can be both. One of the examples that you can use is the boxer Muhammad Ali. He was firm and a powerful fighter in the boxing ring, but outside of that world, he was a philanthropist who worked very passionately for social justice causes.

Another example could be Martin Luther King Jr., who focused on peaceful demonstrations in response to the violence that African Americans faced for generations. Rather than fighting and encouraging brutality, Martin Luther King Jr. sought to support civil rights by peaceful protest. If you can connect a role model with your son's current interests, whether it is sports or music, that can go even further to motivate and inspire your son. You might even reference people in your own lives that are close to your son and your family. Someone like a brother, an uncle, or even a grandfather can serve as a role model for your son to represent themselves.

You might even ask your son about a person they look up to and build a discussion around this person and how your son can adopt some of their positive practices into his life. Open communication is the foundation for making improvements and evolving in your life. The last thing you want is for your son to feel ashamed or embarrassed about themselves. Framing it within a discussion allows them to see that they aren't being attacked for any poor decisions or mistakes. Instead, they can see it as room for them to grow and improve as a person, which is a work in progress for everyone and not just boys and young people.

Chapter 7:
The Joy of Raising Sons

Raising children means that you are raising the future generation. For a parent, this is a huge responsibility and is both terrifying and incredible at the same time. There are so many joys to raising a child. It is challenging work, and no parent in the world has had an easy time raising their children. The decision to have children is costly and is also going to take a lot of personal sacrifices. But having children will also teach you so many lessons that you would never have learned otherwise about yourself, family, and fostering strong relationships that last. Having children means that you accept that you will fail at some point because life will throw so many challenges at you as you raise your sons into men, and it will be extremely emotional.

For parents who are raising both boys and girls, different joys come with raising a particular gender. Yet, the focus is not on the fact that the child is a boy or a girl, but more so that the child is exploring the world around them and finding their place within it. This is an exciting time for parents to see how their children are evolving to take the lessons they have been taught and raise the bar to exceed expectations.

For Amy, a new mother of twins, she found this to be especially true. She had initially been so excited about the fact that she was giving birth to twins, in addition to the anxiety and panic about being a first-time mother. While everyone around her seemed to fixate on the fact that she had twins, Amy became increasingly familiar with the fact that her children were worlds apart from each other. They were unique in their way and had their passions in life. While the rest of the world grouped them as an identical set, Amy was more than aware of their individuality and strived to support their diversity and uniqueness. Being a twin is exceptional, yet people commonly tend to generalize and forget that two very different people are present. Amy learned this as a mother and quickly implemented this as she raised her twins. Her older twin, Max, loved dancing and would go on to become a professional choreographer. Maya, his younger twin sister, became a high school science teacher. They were both so different, despite being twins. Even for parents who don't have twins, it is essential to remember the individuality of your son and celebrate this fact.

As a parent, you automatically become a role model and a mentor to your children, even if that wasn't what you had intended to begin with. For parents, their children have been in the pipeline to get them to explore outside of their comfort zones as they try to keep up and relate to their children. Their children have unexpectedly opened them up to new experiences and learning opportunities.

Knowing that you are raising your children to grow up and eventually leave your home can be heartbreaking for parents. You are essentially preparing your child to move on from relying on you the moment they are born. But this also means that it is an immense joy to see your children thrive and flourish after years of working to mold and shape them into the best versions of themselves. It is advantageous to see your child become a full-grown adult and navigate their way through life independently. It makes every sacrifice worth it, in the end, knowing that you have raised a functioning member of society who is striving to leave the world in a better place than they had found it. Motivation, for so many parents, lies in the fact that you are raising the next generation.

Mothers eventually learn that they are not just raising boys. They are raising future husbands and fathers who will undergo immense trials and tribulations that they have been through themselves. Having children who look to you as the means to survive and then watching them grow and mature to be able to make their own life-altering decisions is a bittersweet and beautiful thing. There is an immense sense of pride and a strong sense of sadness as children grow so quickly. For many parents raising young boys, it is almost like the changes happen overnight.

Unconditional love is a remarkable thing. It keeps parents going, even when there are days where they can't seem to have any peace throughout the daily chaos of their children. There will be so many days for parents of young boys where you constantly worry and feel incredibly frustrated. There will be moments where you simply want to quit and shut yourself away from the world because you seem to be going nowhere. Despite all of these frustrations, the exciting thing for most parents is that the most challenging part about parenting is not the moments of anger or strife. Commonly, the most difficult part about raising sons is coming to terms with the fact that your child is growing every single day at such a rapid pace, for boys, especially, who seem to be children one day until puberty hits them out of nowhere. By then, they are already burgeoning adults.

The biggest takeaway from this book is that trust is the foundation for a good connection between parents and their children. Having confidence allows children to be open and honest about their feelings and emotions. And while it was formerly acceptable for boys to bottle up their feelings and hide away the complexities they were dealing with internally, this has undoubtedly changed in modern times. These days, boys' emotionality and feelings are prioritized to protect their mental health and well-being. In the contemporary era, boys no longer have to conform to society's standards of masculinity. Toxic masculinity is incredibly harmful to boys worldwide because it encourages one extremely unrealistic idea of masculinity that is not attainable. Toxic masculinity celebrates aggressive, "macho" men who lack respect for women and their boundaries. As a parent, it is your responsibility to combat these ideas so that your son doesn't fall into the trap of such tropes that can harm their self-esteem and self-worth. Instead, celebrate the differences and unique perspectives that your son brings. Rather than forcing him to fit into a specific mold or standard, allow him to flourish and create his path.

There is also so much room for growth from both parents and their children alike. Many parents have gotten off on the wrong foot with their kids and are trying to pick up the pieces and rebuild a strong connection and relationship from scratch. This can be extremely difficult as both parties are harboring negative emotions and attempting to move past them. For parents in this situation, the desire to develop a close relationship with their son is already a step in the right direction and a vast improvement overall. But be prepared to be met with resistance and disinterest because sons can be difficult to communicate with. Yet with persistence, you will be able to leave a lasting impression on him. While kids and teens can harbor negative feelings and hold resentment for a long time, they can also forgive. If you are attempting to make right any wrongs with your children, there is a light at the end of the tunnel, and there is a future where you and your child can value each other as a parent and son should. It simply takes time.

The tips that are provided in this book are only practical when they are applied to everyday life. And while it can undoubtedly be overwhelming with the number of different proposed strategies in this book, remember that the backbone of effective parenting is love and trust. Trust yourself to make the right decisions for your children, especially if it is driven by love. Trust your relationship with your child and believe that you can strengthen your relationship by taking the time to get to know them. Always remember that your son is a human being and is going through the same hardships and challenges that you probably have gone through as well, which is why empathy will always go a very long way.

Remember to stay persistent as you raise your son and shape them into the successful and good-hearted man he should be. Despite all the challenges, good parenting will always pay off handsomely. The world is full of endless possibilities, and as you equip your son with the knowledge on how to navigate the world, open his eyes to the dreams that he can achieve with hard work and the right mindset. Be a positive force in your son's life by taking his dreams seriously and celebrating his achievements as your own.

With your son, aim to reach the potential that is buried beneath all of the layers. Societal norms will continue to stifle and enforce self-expression but having parents who fully accept and celebrate their sons will go a long way. Societal institutions like schools and the workforce will only limit your son. Take advantage of mentors and role models so that your son always has a positive force in all of these environments. Parents are the driving force behind a positive atmosphere within the household because they can control the message they want to send out to their children. Rather than focusing on traditional stereotypes that require our sons to be "macho," choose to foster self-assuredness in their abilities and choices and convey to your sons that it is perfectly acceptable to be themselves, no matter what society may tell them.

Please Leave a
1-click Review!

I would be incredibly thankful if you could take just 60 seconds to write a brief review on Amazon or the platform of purchase, even if it's just a few sentences!

Conclusion

When it comes to raising sons, having the right game plan is essential to ensure that they are on the right path of development. Kids are effectively a blank slate when they are born, and it becomes the parents' responsibility to equip their son with the knowledge and guidance that they will need to succeed in life. However, it is essential to remember that the basis of such success is a good parent and son relationship, which many parents tend to struggle with. This guidebook shares all of the tips and tricks to develop an honest and trustworthy relationship based on mutual respect between parent and son. By having this foundation, a parent will guide their son and mold them into the best version of themselves. The core values that they will instill from a young age will follow their son throughout his life and continue its cycle as he becomes an adult and parent. Mental health is emphasized for both parent and son to ensure the best environment possible to nurture your son's individuality and uniqueness. For the complete guide on how to progress from this guide which is targeted at boys aged two to twelve years old, refer to *Raising Teen Boys* and *Raising Teen Girls*. Those looking for a guide to raising girls between the age two to twelve years old refer to the accompanying book entitled *Raising Girls*.

Other Books You'll Love!

1. Raising Boys in Today's Digital World: Proven Positive Parenting Tips for Raising Respectful, Successful and Confident Boys

2. Raising Girls in Today's Digital World: Proven Positive Parenting Tips for Raising Respectful, Successful and Confident Girls

3. Raising Kids in Today's Digital World: Proven Positive Parenting Tips for Raising Respectful, Successful and Confident Kids

4. The Child Development and Positive Parenting Master Class 2-in-1 Bundle: Proven Methods for Raising Well-Behaved and Intelligent Children, with Accelerated Learning Methods

5. Parenting Teens in Today's Challenging World 2-in-1 Bundle: Proven Methods for Improving Teenagers Behaviour with Positive Parenting and Family Communication

6. Life Strategies for Teenagers: Positive Parenting, Tips and Understanding Teens for Better Communication and a Happy Family

7. Parenting Teen Girls in Today's Challenging World: Proven Methods for Improving Teenagers Behaviour with Whole Brain Training

8. Parenting Teen Boys in Today's Challenging World: Proven Methods for Improving Teenagers Behaviour with Whole Brain Training

9. 101 Tips For Helping With Your Child's Learning: Proven Strategies for Accelerated Learning and Raising Smart Children Using Positive Parenting Skills

10. 101 Tips for Child Development: Proven Methods for Raising Children and Improving Kids Behavior with Whole Brain Training

11. Financial Tips to Help Kids: Proven Methods for Teaching Kids Money Management and Financial Responsibility

12. Healthy Habits for Kids: Positive Parenting Tips for Fun Kids Exercises, Healthy Snacks, and Improved Kids Nutrition

13. Mini Habits for Happy Kids: Proven Parenting Tips for Positive Discipline and Improving Kids' Behavior

14. Good Habits for Healthy Kids 2-in-1 Combo Pack: Proven Positive Parenting Tips for Improving Kids Fitness and Children's Behavior

15. The Safe and Responsible Teenager 2-in-1 Combo Pack: Better Communication, Internet and Cell Phone Safety for Teens, Plus Budgeting and Finance for Children

16. Tips for #CollegeLife: Powerful College Advice for Excelling as a College Freshman

17. The Career Success Formula: Proven Career Development Advice and Finding Rewarding Employment for Young Adults and College Graduates

18. The Motivated Young Adult's Guide to Career Success and Adulthood: Proven Tips for Becoming a Mature Adult, Starting a Rewarding Career and Finding Life Balance

19. Bedtime Stories for Kids: Short Funny Stories and poems Collection for Children and Toddlers

20. Guide for Boarding School Life

21. The Fear of The Lord: How God's Honour Guarantees Your Peace

Your Free Gift!

As a way of saying thank you for Your purchase, I have included a gift that you can download at TCEC publishing .com

Facebook Community

I will like to invite you to our Facebook community group to visit this link and simply click the join group.

https://www.facebook.com/groups/397683731371863

This is a private group where parents, teachers, and carers can learn, share tips, ask questions, discuss and get valuable content about raising and parent modern children. It is a very supportive and encouraging group where valuable content, free resources, and exciting discussion about parenting are being shared. You can use this to benefit from social media. You will be learning a lot from school teachers, experts, counselors, new and experienced parents, and stay updated with our latest releases.

See you there!

References

[1] https://cchp.ucsf.edu/sites/g/files/tkssra181/f/SelfEsteem_en0710.pdf

[2] https://www.theseus.fi/bitstream/handle/10024/50239/Anttila_Marianna_Saikkonen_Pinja.pdf

[3] https://ijcat.com/archives/volume5/issue2/ijcatr05021006.pdf

[4] https://www.harvey.k-state.edu/family-and-consumer-sciences/family_and_child_development/documents/CommunicatingwTeenTrust.pdf

[5] https://www.researchgate.net/publication/283721084_Early_Reading_Development

[6] https://www.understood.org/en/friends-feelings/empowering-your-child/building-on-strengths/download-hands-on-activity-to-identify-your-childs-strengths

[7] https://www.wfm.noaa.gov/pdfs/ParentingYourTeen_Handout1.pdf

[8] https://www.helpguide.org/articles/depression/parents-guide-to-teen-depression.htm?pdf=13027

[9] https://www2.ed.gov/parents/academic/help/adolescence/adolescence.pdf

[10] http://centerforchildwelfare.org/kb/prprouthome/Helping%20Your%20Children%20Navigate%20Their%20Teenage%20Years.pdf

[11] https://www.childrensmn.org/images/family_resource_pdf/027121.pdf

[12] https://educationnorthwest.org/sites/default/files/developing-empathy-in-children-and-youth.pdf

[13] http://drkateaubrey.com/wp-content/uploads/2016/02/Parenting-Your-Strong-Willed-Child.pdf

[14] https://www.researchgate.net/publication/263227023_Family_Time_Activities_and_Adolescents'_Emotional_Well-being
[15] https://parenting-ed.org/wp-content/themes/parenting-ed/files/handouts/communication-parent-to-child.pdf
[16] https://www.wikihow.mom/Trust-Your-Teenager
[17] https://www.statmodel.com/download/Meeus,%20vd%20Schoot,%20Klimstra%20&.pdf
[18] https://www.nap.edu/resource/19401/ProfKnowCompFINAL.pdf
[19] http://www.delmarlearning.com/companions/content/1418019224/AdditionalSupport/box11.1.pdf
[20] http://resources.beyondblue.org.au/prism/file?token=BL/1810_A
[21] https://exeter.anglican.org/wp-content/uploads/2014/11/Listening-to-children-leaflet_NCB.pdf
[22] https://www.researchgate.net/publication/312600262_Creative_Thinking_among_Preschool_Children
[23] https://www.gutenberg.org/files/15114/15114-pdf.pdf
[24] https://discovery.ucl.ac.uk/id/eprint/1522668/1/Thesis%20Moulton%20V%20281016.pdf
[25] https://www.bda.uk.com/foodfacts/healthyeatingchildren.pdf
[26] http://www.tuskmont.org/uploads/1/7/7/2/17728377/follow_the_child_trust_the_child.pdf
[27] https://www.apa.org/pi/families/resources/develop.pdf
[28] https://extension.colostate.edu/docs/pubs/consumer/10249.pdf
[29] https://www.empoweringparents.com/article/risky-teen-behavior-can-you-trust-your-child-again/
[30] http://www.wecf.eu/download/2018/05%20May/WSSPPublicationENPartC-MHMchapter.pdf

www.ingramcontent.com/pod-product-compliance
Lightning Source LLC
Chambersburg PA
CBHW070105120526
44588CB00032B/1090